A History of Mennonite Workers' Peace Mission since the Korean War (1951 – 1971)

DANIEL CHOI

DEDICATION

I dedicate this book to

Dallas Voran	Dale Weaver	Verne Kohls
Mrs. V. Kohls	Eva Haraharger	Robert Lee
J. Harold Yoder	Mrs. H. Yoder	Adam Ewert
Katherine Dyck	Lois Kuhns	Kaward Burkholder
Eldon Warkentin	Enest Raber	ClaraEshleman
Harry Harms	Mrs. H. Harms	Omar Lantz
Woodrow Ramseyer	Merle Springer	Valentin Yutzy
Fern Hershberger	Arlene Sitler	Donald Klippenstein
Mrs. Klippnshtein	Bertha Korneslson	Margaret Wiens
James Hostetler	Helen Tieszen	Kenneth Brunk
Mrs. K. Brunk	M. Joseph Smucker	Ketherine Friesen
Robert Gerber	Lloyd Miller	Leland Voth
Mrs. L. Voth	Arlene Zimmerman	Ruth Keim
Jacob M. Klassen	Mrs. J. Klassen	Daniel Roth
Irma Dyck	Tina Letkeman	John Zook
Mrs. J. Zook	Allen Litwiller	Elton Sutter
Mabel Brunk	Esther Thiessen	Roy Bauman
Dorothy Hoover	Rydia Schlabach	Paul Hochstetler
Eugene Dick	Harding Derksen	Karl Bartsch
Mrs. K. Bartsch	John Slotter	Walter Rutt
Mrs. W. Rutt	Lyle Troyer	Leon Sommers
Mark Miller	Lloyd Ramseyer	Mrs. L. Ramseyer
Henry Goossen	Mrs. H. Goossen	Gary Marner
Mrs. G. Marner	Alfred Geiser	Andrew Leatherman
Mrs. A. Leatherman.	John R. Dyck	Mrs. R. Dyck

MCC USA/Canada and MCC Korean workers, who built a messianic peace mission as peace messengers in South Korea.

Daniel (SangJin) Choi / Mennonite Pastor
-Fourth Street Community Fellowship
-Founder & Executive Director, Action for Peace through Prayer and Aid

KOREAN WAR AND "FATHERS OF WAR ORPHANS"

North Korea's attack on South Korea led to the Korean War, resulting in tens of thousands of victims and war orphans. Even missionaries who entered South Korea and were engaged in missionary work were repatriated or forced to flee to the South, where North Korea had not yet attacked. Because of the war, no one could enter South Korea and take care of the orphans who were bleeding and suffering without U.N. approval.

At this time, they begged the U.N. Secretary-General and the U.S. Secretary-General to come to Korea directly, distribute relief supplies directly to war orphans, and allow them to take care of them. These were peace workers of the Mennonite community, called one of the historical peace churches. At the suggestion of the U.S. Secretary-General and the U.N. Secretary-General, Dallas Voran, a member of the Mennonite community, took his first step into Korea as a U.N. employee.

Following Dallas Voran, 77 volunteers came to Korea for 20 years and successfully implemented large-scale relief projects, vocational schools, hospital missions, teacher education, and economic self-support policies. Among the volunteer activities they did was reconciliation between Korea and Japan, which had long been in conflict at the time. As the first civilian-based conflict transformation program in Korea, this program was very professional and successful. Many young Korean and Japanese participants in this program shed tears and shared forgiveness and love for each other.

In addition, since the Korea mission, Mennonite peace volunteers have helped North Korea. They are engaged in various activities, such as North Korean relief and inter-Korean reconciliation.

It describes the impressive activities, conflict resolution, and peacebuilding wisdom Mennonite peace workers displayed during the Korean War, commonly called the "fathers of orphans."

CONTENTS

ACKNOWLEDGMENTS

Many people contributed their ideas and encouraged me to complete my work. They were former MCC workers who served in Korea for peace. I was introduced to many people at the reunion meeting, held on July 1-2, 1994, at Canadian Mennonite Bible College (CMBC). So much credit must be given to my special friends – Helen R. Tieszen, John Zook, Mrs. Rosemary Zook, and Mabel Brunk – who gave me warm-hearted encouragement and proofread my work.

When I was a student at Associated Mennonite Biblical Seminary in 1995, Dr. John Howard Yoder and Mrs. Yoder invited me to their house. At that time, they had been in a car accident, and Dr. Yoder's leg was in a cast, so he had to use a cane to walk. Mrs. Yoder also had to use a walker to move about. Dr. Yoder asked what my purpose was in studying at the Mennonite School. I said I would like to study the Mennonite Peace movement to apply it to the Korean Peninsula and promote racial harmony. During this conversation, he mentioned the Korean Civil War. This was when Mennonite leaders gathered to discuss how to help war orphans and provide material aid to the Korean starving population. He also mentioned that he had been praying for peaceful resolutions to the Korean conflict since the Korean Civil War. He said that many peace-loving Mennonite people applied to work in Korea. Inspired by Dr. Yoder, I decided to compile their remarkable work and share it with Koreans. Therefore, I started collecting materials from previous Mennonite workers in Korea.

Foremost, I would like to express my special thanks to Dr.

Chul-Ha Han, Chancellor of Asia United Theological University, who planted a vision of the evangelization of Asia in my mind, Dr. Young-Shik Choue, Chancellor of Kyung Hee University, Ambassador Dr. Pyo-Wook Han, and other professors at The Graduate Institute of Peace Studies (GIP), who helped me open my eyes to the vision of an international peace-messenger.

Special thanks must also be extended to the archivists of Goshen College in Goshen, Indiana. They have given me their generous help and time in researching historical documents of Korea and USA MCC. I must not forget to give thanks to the following professors: Dr. Ted Koontz, Dr. Willard M. Swartley, and Dr. Ben Ollenburger from Associated Mennonite Biblical Seminary, Dr. John Paul Lederach and Dr. Vernon E. Jantzi from Eastern Mennonite University, Dr. Willbert R. Shenk from Fuller Theological Seminary, and Dr. Chong-Keun Yoon from James Madison University. They read my paper, shared their thoughts, and offered helpful suggestions to improve my work.

I am extremely grateful to Dr. Norman Kraus and Dr. Myron Augsburger. They spent many hours proofreading my work and, most importantly, providing generous encouragement. A special word of thanks also extends to the families of Dr. Jin-Chul Kim and Rev. Dong-Soo Lee. They helped me with their superior computer skills and faithful prayers.

Finally, I would like to express my thanks to the Korean-American church for its material and spiritual sponsorship, to my family who lives in Seoul, Korea, especially to my mother and wife who always encourage me through prayer, and I would like to acknowledge that this work is the fruit of Rev. Lee-Bong Kim and Rev. Yoon-Shik Lee, fellows of the Abba Shalom Community in Korea.

INTRODUCTION

The Korean church celebrated the Centennial Year of Protestant Missions in 1984. On September 20, 1884, the first Presbyterian missionary, Horace N. Allen, M.D., arrived in Korea. On Easter morning, April 5, 1885, the first Methodist missionary, the Rev. Henry G. Appenzeller arrived in Inchon, Korea. [1] With explosive growth, Protestant Christians have reached approximately 12,000,000 along with the 60th anniversary of the Mennonite Mission in Korea. Few people know about this celebration event, so I am writing this book to share this marvelous story not only for Koreans but for all people alike.

Dallas Voran became the first MCC worker in Korea in 1951. Before working in Korea, he served in Cyprus from 1943-1946 during the Second World War. He also served four years in China from 1946-1950, during which he received loans from the Church World Service's Office in Shanghai.[2]

---

[1] *Korean Church Growth and Explosion,* edited by Ro Bong-Rin and Marlin L. Nelson, Taichung: Asia Theological Association and Seoul: Word of Life Press, 1983, p.184.

[2] MCC *Korea 15th Anniversary* published in 1968 reported the first worker as follows: "In October of 1950 the first MCC worker was granted permission to enter Korea." I think this number '1950' was a typing mistake of '1951'. According to *The Mennonite Weekly Review* published on November 30, 1950, nobody was permitted to enter Korea in 1950: "The MCC has been participating in meetings with other relief agencies and governmental officials to lay plans for relief in Korea... It does not yet permit the operation of

MCC Korea 15th Anniversary published in 1968 reports on the first worker as follows: I believe that Dallas Voran was granted permission to enter Korea by the United Nations Civil Assistance Command (UNCAC) in October 1950.[3] However, due to the Korea war, no one was allowed to visit Korea in 1950 even though permission was granted to Dallas Voran. According to The Mennonite Weekly Review published on November 30, 1950, nobody could enter Korea in 1950: "The MCC has been participating in meetings with other relief agencies and government officials to lay plans for relief in Korea… It does not yet permit American relief personnel in the field."

In Dallas Voran's Letter to J.N. Byler, October 26, 1951, he mentioned that he would leave for Pusan, where the United Nations Civil Assistance Command (UNCAC) is located, at 10:30 tomorrow morning. Looking at the letter between Voran and Byler, Voran wrote it on October 26, 1951. He said he would arrive in Pusan the next day, October 27, 1951.[4]

American relief personnel in the field." In the *Dallas Voran's Letter to J.N. Byler*, October 26, 1951, he mentioned that he will take off for Pusan in Korea where United Nations Civil Assistance Command (UNCAC) is located, at 10:30 tomorrow (27th) morning. See *Dallas Voran's Letter to J.N. Byler*, October 26, 1951, found in the file entitled "Dallas Voran, 1951," in the MCC Correspondence Files (IX-6-3), Archives of the Mennonite Church, Indiana. Choi Sang-Jin and Dallas Voran, *Personal Letters*, November 27, 1996. Sang Jin Choi and Dallas Voran, Personal Letters, November 27, 1996.

[3] In his letter to Mr. Glenn Esh, MCC staff, Akron, Pennsylvania, Voran mentioned he received the answer in which the Secretary-General of UN approved his working with UNCAC from Department of Army, Washington. See *Dallas Voran's Letter to Glenn Esh*, October 26, 1951, found in the file entitled "Dallas Voran, 1951." Clyde L. Hyssong, Major General, U.S. Army, Retired, sent Dallas Voran's Memorandum to the Assistant Chief of Staff, G-1, GHQ, United Nations Command, Tokyo. General Hyssong was the chief of mission at the United Nations Korean Reconstruction Agency, Tokyo. See *Glenn Hyssong's Letter to the Assistant Chief of Staff, G-1, GHQ*, October 22, 1951, found in the file entitled "Dallas Voran, 1951."

[4] According to personal communication, SangJin Choi and Dallas Voran, November 27, 1996, his previous experience with MCC was three years in Cypurus (1943-46) during World War II and four years in China (1946-50) during which time he was on loan to Church World Service's office in Shanghai.

In October 1951, after more than half a century of Protestant missions, the first Mennonite Central Committee (MCC) worker, Dallas Voran, was granted permission to enter Korea and arrived in Pusan on October 27. He worked under the administration of the United Nations serving indirectly as an MCC representative.[5] His recollection of going to Korea is as follows:

> "When the North invaded the South on June 25, 1950, their forces advanced very far into the South, including Taegu, and threatened Pusan. The United Nations Civil Assistance Command (UNCAC) had difficulty evacuating foreign civilians. The UNCAC forbade civilian entry. This inability to enter Korea was the reason MCC asked me to go to Japan to find an alternative way into Korea. This was so we would have someone on the ground when it was possible to start a relief and reconstruction program after the war."[6]

In late 1952, Voran left the MCC to take a full-time position

---

See Dallas Voran's Letter to J.N. Byler, October 26, 1951, found in the file entitled "Dallas Voran, 1951," in the MCC Correspondence Files (IX-6-3), Archives of the Mennonite Church, Indiana. SangJin Choi and Dallas Voran Personal Letters, November 27, 1996.

[5] Personal communication, SangJin Choi and Dallas Voran, "UNKRA also had Voluntary Agency Liaison Officer in their Pusan office – Miss Augusta Mayerson. She offered me a job as her assistant. I asked MCC if they would release me. They agreed. That was how I got my first salaried job and gave up the MCC monthly allowances that I had been on most of the time since 1943. That was how I was able to stay in Korea for four years, until July 1955. By that time, I realized that I was hooked on international work, so I went back to school (for a Master's in Social Work from the University of Minnesota) and spent the rest of my working career in international development with the United States Agency for International Development (USAID)."

[6] Personal communication, SangJin Choi and Robert Lee, November 14, 1996. "Erine Raber got married to Mary Raber, who was already in Korea with the Methodist Mission, in Posudong Church in Pusan, October 1953," personal communication, SangJin Choi and Mary Raber, December 22, 1996.

with the United Nations Korean Reconstruction Agency (UNKRA) to further develop MCC missions in Korea. The UNKRA was a non-military agency of the UN with no connection to the UNCAC, the military agency. This made it possible for Voran to volunteer for MCC while working at UNKRA.[7]

While working full-time at UNKRA and serve MCC in his spare time, Voran lost sight of serving at MCC. He fell into all his international work at UNKRA. He worked very hard for UNKRA, but soon realized he had forgotten his social work at MCC. Voran then returned to school for a Master's in Social Work at the University of Minnesota. After graduating, he devoted the rest of his career to international development with the United States Agency for International Development (USAID).[8]

With the assistance of J. N. Byler in May and June 1952 and Dale Nebel, director of the MCC's Far Eastern Area Office mainly in Java now better known as Indonesia, Formosa now better known as Taiwan, and Japan, in November 1952, the field survey was completed which would be used by Dallas Voran in the future. Although Voran had completed surveys that were very beneficial for him, he had many problems beginning his missionary work. This is because "The United Nations Military in August liberalized its control by issuing "Standing Operating Procedure (SOP) 16" which permits voluntary agencies to operate in Korea under limited conditions."[9]

Because he became a full-time worker at the UNKRA, Voran's resignation from the MCC permitted the MCC to send Dale Weaver and Ernie Raber to Korea. Dale set up the first MCC unit in Taegu with the help of Voran and became the first director in Korea, while Ernie opened an office in Pusan to receive relief supplies.[10] Dale Nebel also was in Korea most of

---

[7] Personal communication, SangJin Choi and Dallas Voran.

[8] Sang Jin Choi and Dallas Voran Personal Letters, November 27, 1996.

[9] *Annual Report of MCC*, November 30, 1952, Relief Section, Page 15

[10] Personal communication, SangJin Choi and Robert Lee, November 14, 1996.

1953 and 1954 in order to work with Dale Weaver, even though his assignment was to the MCC's regional office in Osaka, Japan. L. Robert Kohls, Norma Kohls, J. Harold Yoder, Patricia S. Yoder, Eva Harshbarger, Robert Lee, Lois Kuhns Ramseyer, Katherine Dyck, Adam Emert, Eldon Warkentine, and Howard Burkholder also were among the earliest personnel who arrived in 1953.

During the twenty-year period from 1951 to 1971, MCC sent 77 workers to Korea.8 MCC workers played a significant role in enabling Korean people to support themselves, basing their work to the biblical themes of relief and service to the alien, the orphan, and the widow (Deut. 14:29).[11] Two of these 77 workers lost their lives in an accident in Korea: Bertha Kornelson and Katherine Dyck both drowned on August 2, 1956, when they were swept off a rock where they were sitting by a huge wave.[12]

During the war, MCC's service work was evident in Korea's rebuilding process. Despite their devoted work, however, we could not find any records of MCC activity in the Korean church mission history books. Some reasons why there wasn't much MCC activity in Korean churches are
as follows: First, MCC worked mainly in two areas: Gyeong San and Taegu. Although they had workers all over Korea under different organizations, they only had two main offices. Secondly, MCC did not plant churches or do pastoral ministry, because MCC was very concentrated on service and mission

---

[11] Reports *and Statistics for 1971* reported 74 MCC overseas workers serving in Korea. However, this statistic omitted two Canadian workers, Walter Rutt and Mrs. Gladys Rutt. The total number of workers at MCC was therefore 76. See *Reports and Statistics from 1963 to 1965*, Overseas Services; *The Canadian Mennonite*, April 12, p.8.

[12] "Bertha Kornelson's body is buried on the farm where MCC had the Mennonite Vocational School for high school orphan boys, in Daegu. Katherine Dick's body was sent home by her parents. I think they were the only two who lost their lives while working as MCC workers in Korea. It was a tragic day, especially since Bertha and I had traveled to Korea together and were working in the Pusan Children's Hospital together," personal communication, SangJin Choi and Margaret Wiens November 9, 1996.

arms which were very necessary at the time.[13] Thirdly, MCC withdrew most of its workers by 1971 due to Korea's economic growth, shifting MCC's attention toward the peace mission in Africa.

Furthermore, for a twenty-five-year period (1971-1996), few Mennonites were actively involved in church work in Korea, notwithstanding Helen R. Tieszen in Seoul (1974-1992), from where she maintained communications with the MCC and the COM (the Canadian Mennonite agency). Overall, most Korean-related MCC materials are kept in the Mennonite Church Archives at Goshen College in Goshen, Indiana. In addition, there are others such as MCC headquarters in Akron, Pennsylvania, and Canadian Mennonite Biblical College (CMBC) in Manitoba, Canada. Also, all materials were written in English, making it very difficult for Korean authors to write Korean church history.[14]

Therefore, I have two purposes for my study: one is to inform people about the MCC worker's devoted mission work. For this purpose, I added the study of the Korean War historical background and North American MCC's reactions to Chapter 1. In Chapter 2, I studied the analysis of MCC's programs: material aid programs, education programs, some projects for economic "self-support" such as economic justice policies, and the healing mission program. MCC's reconciliation programs between Japan and Korea are discussed in Chapter 3. In Chapter 4, I have several suggestions for developing a peacebuilding project for Korea through MCC. I mentioned a theoretical

---

[13] Korea *Director, J.R. Dyck's Letter to the Governor of the North Kyung San,* May 26, 1969, found in the file entitled "Mennonite Vocational School 1954-1970," File 41, in the MCC Korean File (IX-34), Archives of the Mennonite Church, Goshen, Indiana. *The Report on the Kyung San Vocational School for Orphan Boys Submitted to the United Nations Women's Guild,* January, 1995 and *The Asia Foundation,* January, 1956, found in the same file, also demonstrated it as follows: "Although this school receives continuous support from the Mennonites of North America, we are not a missionary group and we do not teach "Mennonite" to our students..."

[14] I was very grateful to discover the existence of the archives to properly document and honor the efforts of Mennonite workers in Korea.

approach toward religious peace-building, the necessity of the messianic peace mission toward the Asian structural conflict and its resolution, and Jubilee theology as a means of humanity restoration between North and South Korea in Chapter 5. In Chapter 6, I added my comparison study in Chapter 4 of two Asian peace movements 'traditions based on nonviolence: the Korean March First Movement (1991) against Japanese colonial rule and Gandhi's Satyagraha Campaign (April 6, 1919) against the British colonial government 's policy of the Rowlatt Bills.

The second purpose of this study is to honor 77 Mennonite peace workers who did a marvelous job in Korea. This was an arduous task because there weren't many written records. I joyfully added their name, position, and terms in the Appendix in honor of their hard work. During my time
of research, I was given the opportunity to present my study project at the MCC East Coast Conference in 1998. I also reported it at the MCC Headquarters Chapel to all headquarter staff in 1999, in Akron, Pennsylvania.

My hope in contributing this work is to build a bridge between the Asian conflicts and the messianic peace mission. I pray and hope many people will participate in the rewarding messianic peace mission. This is like the MCC workers in Korea took part in the establishment of religious peacebuilding efforts in Asia.

1

THE KOREAN WAR
AND MCC'S REACTIONS

MCC Headquarters, Gyeongsan, Daegu

The Korean War

Four months after Japan's unconditional surrender on August 15, 1945, the foreign ministers of the United States, the Soviet Union, and the United Kingdom met in a conference in Moscow on December 27 to discuss the trusteeship of Korea. The American-Soviet Joint Commission was to submit "a four-power trusteeship to prepare Korea for its independence within five years"[15] including China. However, the Joint Commission was faced with the dilemma of unresolved details and the anti-trusteeship movement among South Koreans. The U.S. and Soviet Union's Joint Commission disagreed about whether to accept South Korea's opposite opinions on the trusteeship. Because most of the Anti-Trusteeship movement disliked communism, the Soviet Union refused to hear their opinion but the U.S. accepted South Korea's opinion. Finally, in September 1947, the United States brought the Korean problem before the United Nations.[16]

On September 23, 1947, the General Assembly placed the Korean question on its agenda and referred it to the First Political and Security Committee. Two main issues emerged from the discussions by the First Committee on October 28, 1947: (1) participation of elected representatives of the Korean people in the discussion, and (2) withdrawal of the United States and the Soviet troops from Korea.[17] In November 1947, the UN General Assembly also passed a resolution calling for UN-supervised elections throughout Korea. Although the Soviet

---

[15] *U.S. Department of State, Korea, 1945-1948*, p.6 (1945).

[16] *Report of the United Nations Commission on Korea*, General Assembly, Official Record, 4th Sess., 1949, Vol.1(A/936), pp.32-34.

[17] *The Mennonite Weekly Review*, July 6, 1950.

Union and the Korean authorities in the North refused to accept these elections, they were observed under UN observation in the South. On August 10, 1948, Kim Il-Sung became President of the Democratic People's Republic of Korea (DPRK) with the help of the Soviet Union.

However, the conflict between the Soviet Union and the United States continued despite the establishment of the United Nations Commission on Korea. Both countries' military support increased the hostility between North Korea and South Korea. In September 1949, the United Nations Commission on Korea reported the danger of military posturing to the General Assembly.[18]

Finally, on June 25, 1950, North Korea, with assistance from the Soviet Union, attacked South Korea. The Korean War ended on August 8, 1953, with tragic results. According to the Encyclopedia Britannica (1995), South Korean casualties were around 1,313,000 (1,000,000 civilians); Communist casualties were estimated at about 2,500,000 (including 1,000,000 civilians). The United States lost 33,629 dead in action, South Korea lost 47,000, and UN personnel: 3,194; but the estimated losses of the Chinese in action were a staggering 900,000 men, while North Korea suffered losses of 520,000. During the war (1950-1953), 43 percent of Korea's industrial facilities were destroyed and 33 percent of its homes were destroyed.

MCC's Reactions to the Korean War

A review of MCC's responses to the Korean War reveals Mennonites' overwhelming concern for peace.

For the first time on July 6, 1950, *The Mennonite Weekly Review* informed its readers of the Korean War:
Not since V-J Day five years ago has the world experienced such war jitters as were induced by the outbreak of hostilities in

---

[18] *The Mennonite Weekly Review*, August 10, 1950.

Korea last week. Soviet-dominated North Korean forces, equipped with Russian planes and tanks, launched an unexpected attack on South Korea and took the capital city of Seoul after only a few days of fighting. On Friday, President Truman announced American soldiers were sent into action.[19]

From July 6 to December 28, except for three weeks (Oct. 26, Dec. 17 and 21), *The Mennonite Weekly Review* focused exclusively on the Korean War. Editorials on August 10 and October 19 also emphasized MCC 's interest in the Korean situation. MCC had already taken initial steps for relief work and organized a personnel program in Korea:

Already the United Nations is disturbed by the serious refugee problem in Korea. It is estimated that more than a million people are starving and homeless. The situation in Korea and China, too, presents a challenge to the Mennonite people. They should get ready for their relief organizations to move in as soon as conditions permit. Food and medical care, brought in the name of Christ, will come a long way in abolishing the hatred that arises out of the rubble and ruin.[20]

As reported elsewhere in this issue, the Mennonite Central Committee has taken initial steps for relief work in Korea as soon as the government gives permission. Undoubtedly, this action on the part of the Committee will receive the full endorsement of Mennonite churches everywhere. Personnel for the first unit are already organized and likely ready to move into the field on short notice. Now again the terrible destruction in Korea is a challenge to our Christian conscience, and once again it is up to us to show our faith through works.[21]

Secondly, MCC showed its willingness to respond to the Korean War suffering. MCC offered through organized relief channels, to send a medical team consisting of one doctor and two nurses. However, this team which ultimately consisted of

---

[19] *The Mennonite Weekly Review*, October 19, 1950.

[20] *The Annual Report of the MCC*, Chicago, Illinois, December 27-28, 1950, p.3. and personal communication, SangJin Choi and H.R. Tieszen, December 6, 1996.

[21] *The Annual Report of MCC*: Dec. 1, 1950-Nov. 30, 1951, p.41.

only two nurses was supervised by the Unified Command of the United Nations. [22] In October of 1951, Dallas Voran was granted permission to enter Korea. He worked under the United Nations administration serving indirectly as a MCC representative.[23] MCC also participated in meetings with other relief agencies and governmental officials to lay plans for relief in Korea. They developed a committee on American Voluntary Relief to Korea.[24] Thirdly, the MCC Peace Section responded in several ways to the Korean war. A historical conference of North American Mennonites was held by the Peace Section on November 9-12 1950, at Winona Lake, Indiana. "Eighty-seven people, representing MCC constitution groups, met to study Mennonite nonresistant doctrine, its biblical and theological basis, and its implications and applications in today's world. Because of the Korean War, the Peace Section needed a full-time Executive Secretary. J. Harold Shirk, a minister in the United Missionary Church became the first man in that position. During the Korean War, there was, once again, an increase in constitutional support for Peace Section activities. This was equivalent with doubling the support level over the previous four-year period. The Peace Section programs were also changed; they attempted to deal deeper with the causes of war and other forms of conflict.

Lastly, student groups also showed interest in the Korean War. Two student clubs, the Peace Group and the International

---

[22] *The Mennonite Weekly Review*, Nov. 30, 1950.

[23] *The report of the Peace Section to the annual Meeting of the MCC*, Chicago, Illinois, Dec. 27-28, 1950, p.6. An almost immediate result of the Korea war (June 25, 1950) was quick passage of a bill by the government to extend the 1948 Selective Service Act for one year. On August 11 and 17 Universal Military Training (UTM) bills were introduced to the House. The omnibus anti-subversive bill, which was introduced by Senator Pat McCarran on August 10 and finally passed over the President's veto on September 23, contained several amendments to the naturalization laws. At that time, the Department of Defense called for a total armed force of 3,000,000 soldiers. See Ibid., pp.2-4.

[24] *The Annual Report of the MCC*, 1951, p.56; *The Annual Report of the MCC*, 1967, pp.B1-B3.

Relations Club of Bethel College Church in cooperation with the Peace Committee, held a peace lecture in the Student Union room of Memorial Hall at Bethel College on Monday, November 13, 1950 at 8:00 p.m. In-Duk Phak internationally-known lecturer and writer of Korea was invited as the speaker and her topic was "Korea- Its People and Its Future."[25]

---

[25] *The Mennonite Weekly Review*, Nov. 9, 1950, p.4

16

2

MCC'S PROGRAMS IN SOUTH KOREA

MCC Orphanage

Introduction

MCC's policy was based on the biblical injunction to aid the alien, the orphan and the widow (Deut. 14:29). It was a "messianic peace mission" including political, economic, social, and religious dimensions.

<Figure 1>

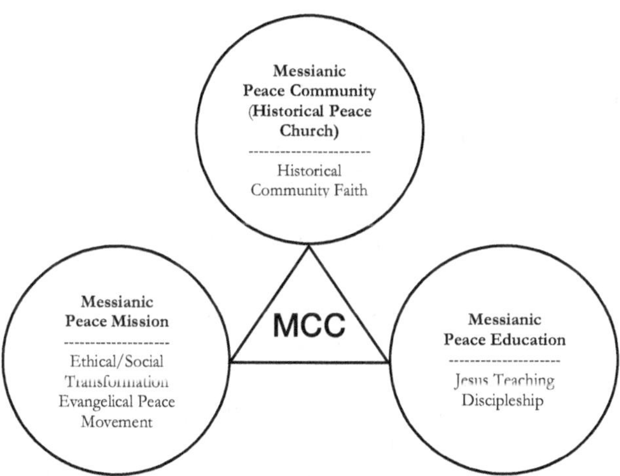

<MCC's Messianic Peace Mission in South Korea>

We can develop Mennonite faith tradition towards peace-building in the view of trifocal messianic peacebuilding: Messianic Peace Community, Messianic Peace Mission, and

Messianic Peace Education. (See Figure 1)

As John Howard Yoder wrote, the peace mission means an experience of the pacifism of the messianic community; MCC's peace movement is a realization of the pacifism of the messianic community. He remarked on the messianic community's pacifism:

> "When we speak of the pacifism of the messianic community, we move the focus of ethical concern from the individual to the human community experiencing in its shared life a foretaste of God's kingdom. It is communal in that it is lived by a covenanting group of men and women. These men and women instruct one another, forgive one another, bear one another's burdens, and reinforce one another's witness."[26]

The various kinds of aid given by MCC including material aid, educational aid, peace movement aid, seconded personnel, economic development aid for self-support, and others are shown in <Figure 2>.

The activities of Mennonite workers can be divided into four periods:

The Preparatory Period (1950-1953)
-preparation of material aid policy during the Korean war
The Fixing Period (1954-1959)
-realization of the basic programs
The Growth Period (1960-1964)
-realization of stable and systematic programs
The Finishing Period (1965-1971)
-withdrawal stage because of Korea's economic growth

---

[26] John Howard Yoder, *Nevertheless: The Varieties and Shortcomings of Religious Pacifism*, Scottdale, PA:Herald Press, 1922, p.135.

<Figure 2>   MCC's Messianic Peacebuilding Program

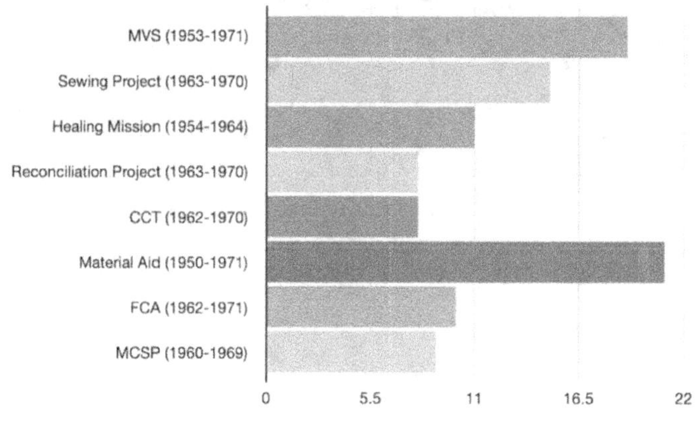

Numbers = service years.
MVS=Mennonite Vocational School
CCT=Christian Child Care Training
FCA=Family Child Assistance
MCSP=Mennonite Community Service Project

1. The Material Aid Program

MCC 's material aid was the most basic response to resolve the serious lack of clothing, food, and shelter caused by the Korean War. MCC Korea located in Taegu was charged with distributing the material aid sent from Mennonites and the U.S. government.

1) Clothing
Following the outbreak of the Korean War, MCC planned to send a trial shipment of 14,627 pounds of clothing in 1950 and

1951. [27] This was the first evidence of MCC's economic assistance for Korea. Clothing was very helpful for refugees during the first winter of war. In fact, MCC sent more clothing to Korea than to any other country. With the end of the Korean War in 1953, poverty in Korea became more serious. In 1956, Korea had 300,000 war widows with 650,000 children and perhaps as many as 150,000 orphans, of which about 50,000 orphans were in institutions.27 In addition, there were 2,000 lepers, 10,000 widows including the elderly and handicapped, and 10,000 sick people in charity and relief hospitals.[28] Also, Typhoon Sara caused extensive damage in 1959. MCC distributed clothing to about 7,000 people in areas worst hit by the typhoon.

<Table 1>   A Five-Year Comparison of Pounds of Clothing

Center	1958	1959	1960	1961	1962
Ephrata	239,511	241,318	271,988	274,186	270,682
N. Newton	122,013	103,110	126,106	135,291	145,204
Kitchener	96,351	111,520	143,665	101,443	99,836
Reedley	27,761	29,615	39,355	39,736	40,317
Yarrow	0	0	21,280	71,418	104,585
Total	**485,536**	**485,663**	**609,394**	**622,074**	**660624**

Korea needed clothing, food and other necessities due to the continuous disasters such as fire, flood, and storm. MCC operated clothing intake centers in Ephrata (PA), North Newton (KS), Kitchener (ON), Reedley (CA), and Yarrow (B.C., from 1960). [29] Sometimes clothing intake includes bedding, shoes,

---

[27] The Annual Report of the MCC, 1951, p.42.
[28] *The Annual Report of the MCC*, 1956, Relief Section, p.6.
[29] Ibid., p.6.

soap, school supplies and bandages.

<Table 1> is a five-year summary of contributions and pounds received at the five clothing centers. [30] A large proportion of the work was handled by volunteer help. A five-year comparison of volunteer –help days is as follows: 1958 – 3,153; 1959 – 3,319; 1960 – 3,528; 1961 – 3,684; 1962 – 4,137.[31] The support of clothing continued for twenty years from 1951 to 1970 as shown in <Table 2>.

<Table 2>   MCC 's Clothing Support (1951-1970)

YEAR	CLOTHING(1b/$)	YEAR	CLOTHING ($)
1951	14, 627 lbs (MCC/US)	1960	$52, 167.40 (")
1952	$26, 129.95 (") *	1961	$64,947.30 (")
1953	$25, 817.47 (") *	1962	$79,590.00 (")
1954	$410, 635.70 (") *	1963	$86,403.00 (")
1955	$295, 310.58 (") **	1964	$82,649.50 (")
1956	165, 053 lbs (")	1965	$65,558.50 (")
1957	$54, 662.75 (US.G)	1966	$111,557.00 (")
	$13, 913.75 (MCC/C)	1967	$90,110.50 (")
1958	$72, 220.37 (US.G)	1968	$73,731.30 (")
	$19, 973.50 (MCC/C)	1969	$121,790.50 (")
1959	$50, 917.70 (MCC/US)	1970	$29,043.50 (")

I have adapted this table from *The Annual Report of the MCC*, 1951-19
* including soap ** including food
US. G- U.S. government   MCC/C – MCC Canada

2) Feeding Station

In 1953 the first food from MCC arrived at the Relief Operation Center located in Daegu. Daegu itself had 70,000 needy people, including refugees, widows, 6,000 children in orphanages, and

---

[30] *The Annual Report of the MCC*, 1954, Relief Section, p.6; *The Annual Report of the MCC*, 1964, p.A-35.
[31] *The Annual Report of the MCC*, 1962, p.A-36.

700 shoe-shine boys. MCC sent milk and rice.[32]

In 1953, MCC proposed a plan, encouraging dimes saving for food relief. It was first announced in the September issue of "A Letter to Boys and Girls." MCC published about 2,500 "Food for Hungry Children" coin cards.[33]

<Table 3>   MCC/U.S. Government's Food Support (1957)

COUNTRY	MCC (lb.)	U.S. Govn't (lb.)
FRANCE	3,187	226,006
GERMANY	53,709	257,000
GREECE	7,484	
HOLLAND	2,951	
JORDAN	17,600	200,000
VIETNAM	34,540	
KOREA	104,136	2,207,618
AUSTRIA	88,283	87,075

This is a rearranged table from *The Annual Report of the MCC*, 1957.

A total of $11,279.92 was received through this project. It was designated to purchase milk and rice for Korean and Jordanian children.[34] As a result of the War, Korea was "the neediest war-stricken area" in the world. According to the Annual Report of the MCC (1955) MCC distributed and assisted over 63,000 people during the year:

The first major distribution was held in Hwachon north of the 38th parallel.[35] Clothing and bedding were distributed to 4,500 people. The second major distribution was held in the

---

[32] Loc. cit.

[33] *The Annual Report of the MCC*, 1953, Relief Section, p.2.

[34] Ibid., p.8.

[35] Ibid., p.7. Abba Shalom Community sponsored by a Canadian Mennonite mission agency also is located in the Whachon area.

Seoul neighborhood of Inchon-Suwon, where 14,000 people were given clothing and bedding. The third distribution outside Daegu was conducted in Gyeongsangnam-do. All these distributions were conducted in cooperation with Korea Church World Service. They furnished transportation, trucking, interpreters, and other assistances in order to make these distributions possible.[36]

The MCC provided 29 relief shipments in 1956 with a net weight of 1,629,859 lbs, and a value of $410,508.99.[37] In 1957 Korea received 2,311,754 lbs, the largest amount of food among other countries as shown in <Table 3>.

In 1959 Korea's births outnumbered deaths by 717,000. This increased population contributed to the economic growth of Korea. In addition, many people lost their homes and farms in the areas worst hit by Typhoon Sara. For this reason, 60,000 people received MCC's emergency food aid. [38] The natural disaster due to Typhoon Sara of 1959 and the political instability due to the April Student Revolution of 1960 followed by the May 1961 military coup detat were the main reasons for the serious hunger crisis of the 1960's. The U.S. government's surplus food sent to Korea by MCC was cut short in 1964. This was because of Korea's economic recovery according to the rapprochement with Japan and the signing of foreign trade agreements. Actually, as radicals have argued, the purpose of U.S. foreign economic aid was not always to solve a real hunger problem, but rather the promotion of its political objectives; that aid in fact strengthened the power of oppressive third world elites.[39] In many cases, U.S. cold war policies of economic aid since the Korean War also were not solely a response of compassion to establish economic justice in the poor countries. Rather, aid was given to support allies' defense and to achieve socio-political dominance or hegemony in the Far East. John

---

[36] *The Annual Report of the MCC*, 1955, Relief Section, p.1.

[37] *The Annual Report of the MCC*, 1956, Purchasing Shipping, p.3.

[38] *The Annual Report of the MCC*, 1959, p.A-8.

[39] Ronald J. Sider, *Rich Christians in an Age of Hunger*, Dallas:Word Publishing, 1990, p.204.

Spaniel commented as follows:

<Table 4>   **MCC's Food Support (1953-1970)**

YEAR	AMOUNTS ($/lb)	YEAR	AMOUNTS ($/lb)
1953	7,501.50	1961	49,665.95 (MCC)
1954	410,635.70*		207,523.23 (US.G)
1955	295,310.58*	1962	37,794.75 (MCC)
1956	253,745 lb. (MCC)		100,799.07 (US.G)
	1,696,588 lb. (US.G)	1963	39,732.35 (MCC)
1957	72,482.92 (MCC)		26,025.30 (US.G)
	162,392.27 (US.G)	1964	60,469.25 (MCC)
1958	77,167.17 (MCC)	1965	72,082.35 (MCC)
	173,544.12 (US.G)	1966	43,822.41 (MCC)
1959	37,913.53 (MCC)	1967	73,153.00 (MCC)
	125,158.78 (US.G)	1968	42,261.04 (MCC)
1960	53,920.07 (MCC)	1969	66,020.10 (MCC)
	302,741.49 (US.G)	1970	33,600.00 (MCC)

I have adapted this table from the MCC's Annual Report, 1953-1971.
*- including of food and others U.S.G – U.S. Government

Indeed, the term "economic aid" was a bit of a misnomer. After 1950 and the outbreak of the Korean War, most economic aid was, in fact, military aid. Even though some of this sum was designated for financial assistance, a significant part was "defense support"; this provided money to sustain allies' economies such as South Korea or South Vietnam, which, without this support, could not maintain their standing armies. Most less-developed nations got nothing.[40] A brief table on how the goods were distributed follows:[41]

Fortunately, MCC analyzed the basic causes of Korea's economic poverty well. MCC distributed material aid in various ways until 1970 when the Korean government's economic development plans were successful. This is shown in <Table

---

[40] John Spanier, *American Foreign Policy Since World War II*, 10th ed., New York: CBS College Publishing, 1985, p. 128.
[41] See *The Annual Report of the MCC*, 1958, Relief Section, p.15.

4>. [42] MCC, as a Christian NGO (Non-Governmental Organization), was based on the principle of God's dominance toward economic justice, not socio-political dominance.

<Table 5>   December 1957 – November 1958

Recipient	Pounds Distributed
119 Institutions	543,101
20 Milk Feeding Stations	263,366
9 Kindergartens	8,360
City Distribution	241,518
Rural Distribution	654,290
Total no. of people 245,536	1,710,645
Total value	**294,146.08 ($)**

3) Christmas Bundles

This Christmas bundles project was very successful. This project was popular with adults and children.42 This project was especially effective for the Christian education of children and youth. Many Christmas bundles were distributed in churches alongside education about Christ's peace message. Beginning in 1954, a total of 7,242 Christmas bundles were sent to Korea.[43] Additionally, in the same year, Korea MCC received 4,500 Christmas food packages through the U.S. government programs of "Operation Reindeer" and "Operation Poinsettia." The food items included butter, shortening, beef and gravy, dry beans, rice, wheat, flour, non-fat dry milk, cheese, and cottonseed oil.[44] In the later period of the Korean War, Korea and Jordan received the largest amount of Christmas bundles. For example, in 1954, Jordan received 1,960 bundles from the U.S.A. and Canada and Korea, 7,242 bundles. In 1955, Korea,

---

[42] *The Annual Report of the MCC,* 1954, Relief Section, p.6.
[43] Ibid., p.6.
[44] Ibid., pp.7-8.

8,028 bundles, and Jordan, 7,678 bundles. [45] MCC sent Christmas bundles to Korea from 1954 to 1069 as <Table 6> indicates.

<Table 6>   MCC's Christmas Bundles (1954-1969)

YEAR	BUNDLES (lb)	YEAR	BUNDLES (lb)
1954	7,242	1962	3,819
1955	8,028		(13,375.00)
1956	?	1963	5,142
1957	12,254	1964	6,137
1958	4,002		(39,572.50)
1959	6,139	1965	2,843
	(56,548.50)	1966	3,504
1960	3,491	1967	3,076
	(19,762.50)	1968	2,400
1961	3,396	1969	3,244
	(11,103.25)		

2. Education

Mennonite Vocational School (MVS) and Child Care Training (CCT) programs were the most important educational programs.

1) Mennonite Vocational School (MVS)

From its beginning, MCC has been concerned about child welfare. The minutes from a 1920 MCC meeting in Chicago stated that "orphanage work may be opened on the field if such seems needed and advisable."[46] MVS was MCC's largest project in Korea. MVS was founded in October 1953 near the town of

---

[45] Ibid., p.6; *The Annual Report of the MCC,* 1955, Relief Section, p.8.
[46] "Monthly Aid Helpers 1000 Children," *The Mennonite,* November 9, 1965, p.698.

GyeongSan in GyeongSangBookDo soon after the Korean War cease-fire.[47] A seventy-eight-acre plot of land was purchased by MCC for the establishment of a vocational school at the junior and high school level for older orphan boys. The site was originally planned by the Japanese (during Japanese rule ending in 1945) to be used as an agricultural college. With the withdrawal of Japanese forces from Korea, many of the twenty-seven buildings were never completed.[48] The first program of this school was the agriculture program. The objectives of the farm program were to provide practical agricultural work experiences for all students, to help with financial support for the educational program, and to serve as a model to neighboring farmers and thus aid in the extension of service.[49] Older orphan boys were taught agriculture and worked in the rice farming project.[50] Christian Children's Fund (CCF) helped in partial support of some of the younger orphan boys, while major support came from MCC "sponsors" in the U.S. and Canada.[51]

In 1954, the MCC Korea began repairing many buildings. They were assisted in the task of rebuilding and repairing the physical plant with grants of money and materials from UNKRA (United Nations Korea Reconstruction Agency), UNCACK (United Nations Civil Assistance Command of Korea), and AFAK (Armed Forces Assistance to Korea- the organization through which the various branches of the U.S. Armed Services in Korea gave aid to schools, hospitals, and other welfare

---

[47] MCC Korea 15th Anniversary Brochure, 1968, p.10.

[48] See The Report on the Gyeongsan Mennonite Vocational School for Orphan Boys Submitted to the United Nations Women's Guild, May, 1955. Also, *The Asia Foundation*, January, 1956.

[49] See *The Report of MVS Conferences* held at MVS, reviewing the present program and suggestions for possible changes on Dec. 1962. This report is found in the file entitled "MVS Reports 1954-1970," Box 1, File 41, in the "MCC Korean Files, AMC."

[50] *The Annual Report of the MCC*, 1953, Relief Section, p.12.

[51] Ibid., p.12.

institutions).[52] The farm project consisted of a physical plant of more than 60 tillable acres of land with some 40 buildings and a native staff of more than 20 people.[53] This included teachers, vocational instructors, farm personnel, laundry workers, cooks, etc.[54]

The objectives of MVS were to teach basic academic skills, vocational skills, and Christian moral education. The technical educational program included academic subjects and training in metal work, printing, carpentry, and agriculture.[55] The Christian moral education program provided spiritual and moral guidance so that a graduate can be a positive and in many cases Christian influence in society.[56] In 1959, the first class of 23 students graduated from MVS.[57] In 1961, MCC bought a house that served as a boys' hostel for graduates from Mennonite Vocational School (MVS) in Daegu. Twenty-one graduates move into the hostel on March 1, 1961. Graduates could live in the hostel until they found a job.[58] In the spring of 1963, Walter Rutt arrived. Walter Rutt was a supervisor for this construction program.[59] Through this project, the principal's house, the Byler dormitory, kitchen, and dormitory rooms for parents were built for MVS, as well as two churches within one mile of the school.[60]

Mennonite Vocational School added a new class in typing in

---

[52] See The Report on the Kyong San Vocational School for Orphan Boys Submitted to the United Nations Women's Guide, May, 1955; *The Annual Report of the MCC*, 1955, Relief Section, p.2.

[53] Ibid., p.12.

[54] *The Annual Report of the MCC*, 1954, p.2.

[55] *The Annual Report of the MCC*, 1956, Relief Section, p.6.

[56] See *MVS Report Operated by MCC Korea*, Feb. 27, 1963, pp. 2-3, found in the title entitled "MVS Reports 1953-1963, Box 1, File 41, in the "MCC Korean Files, AMC."

[57] *The Annual Report of the MCC*, 1959, Relief Section, p.A-8.

[58] *The Annual Report of the MCC*, 1961, Relief Section. P.A-19.

[59] *Reports and Statistics for 1963*, p.A-19.

[60] *Reports and Statistics for 1964*, p.A-24; See "Couple in Middle Sixties Complete Korea Service Term," in *The Canadian Mennonite*, April 12, 1966. Mrs. Gladys Rutt suffered a near fatal illness in 1964. However, the Lord answered and restored her to health. She taught English at MVS.

1965, and a class in electronics – radios and basic electronics, in 1966.[61] In 1967 MVS had changed to a three-year school for only high school age boys.[62] MVS applied for accreditation from the government as a technical high school, because without an official diploma it was difficult to enter or gain employment. This was a very serious problem for MVS students. In December 1962, a conference was held at MVS, reviewing problems and discussing possible changes. The main topics of that conference were government accreditation, clarification of the objectives of the school program, student guidance, teacher-pupil relations, etc. Despite its efforts, MVS was unable to obtain sanction as a technical high school for orphans from the Korean Government. All of MVS's properties and responsibilities were turned over to the MVS national board of directors in July, 1969.[63]

A total of 332 students graduated from MVS. MVS principals include L. Robert Kohls, Kenneth Brunk, John Zook, Leland Voth, and Dong-Keun Lee. The MVS principals include six different principals representing the work done by the individuals in the educational missionary at Mennonite Vocational School for orphan boys. The first principal was Robert Kohls (1953-1956) who came to Korea in 1946 as an American soldier in the United States Armed Forces. During his time in Korea, he became very interested in Korea, especially Koreans. When he returned back to the States, he immediately convinced his wife, Norma, to follow his future dreams in Korea. Robert and Norma Kohls had humble beginnings in a rundown village with a pioneering spirit. Little by little, they found more and more people to help with their mission vision for the orphanage. As the staff of the new school became secure, the school became based upon firm Christian foundations. This demonstrated how to make Christianity practical in everyday life. At first the staff had a lot of troubles

---

[61] *The Annual Report of the MCC*, 1965, p.A-22; *The Annual Report of the MCC*, 1966, p.A-15.
[62] *The Annual Report of the MCC*, 1967, p.A-18.
[63] *The Annual Report of the MCC*, 1969, p.A-11.

receiving a grant in lumber and cement, but they took initiative and began with what they had because they wanted to bring in a handful of boys selectively to train them to be leaders for when other boys finally come. Kohl wrote that, "in the meantime, however, we have gone ahead on our own and are in the process of repairing a few of the buildings so that we may bring in a handful of selected boys who will act as leaders when the rest of the buildings are repaired and the other boys are finally able to come."[64] As the Kohls opened the school with a few select boys, there was a lot of trouble and complaints from the boys about the labor and other work. In the end, they all agreed to work hard to get the school started. Very soon, classes started and money was donated by sponsors in North America every month. Later it became a process to select 40 students through an application process to attend the school.

The Second Principal was Kenneth Brunk (1956-1959) who, from the start, built more and more buildings in addition to those already built. His wife, Twila, was a nurse, so she later became in charge of all the medical care needed in the facility. Because Kenneth Brunk was highly interested in drama, he encouraged students to prepare dramas during Christmas.

Many of the boys really loved this as well as other activities such as ice-skating that Brunk provided for the boys with the many more donations that they received. They also started community development work on the farm fields and other agriculture-related activities. Everything seemed to be working well until a dormitory fire caused three of the dorms to completely burn down. This caused us to salvage items from one of the dorms. After the calamities of the fire ceased, there was a division among students between boys who followed Christian methods and boys who antagonized them. Because of this, Brunk started a point system to encourage better Christian living at the school. Under Brunk, there was the first graduating class.

After Principal Brunk's departure, Leland Voth was interim principal (1959). He became the third principal for a short time.

---

[64] MCC *Activity Report*, October 31, 1953, Verne Robert and Norma Kohl

During his principal tenure, two American boys came to help out at the school, farm and orphanage. Elton, the first of two boys, was known as the "Giant" because he was such a big man. He was in charge of most electrical and repair work at MVS. Allen, the second of the two boys, built and worked on small projects like ping pong tables for MVS boys to enjoy. In addition, he cared for the animals and gardens meticulously to increase production. While Voth was interim principal, he started monthly staff socials. Many changes came about through these meetings such as dormitories being reorganized by age. "A new vocational system was adopted, with first year middle students in the different vocational classes and vocational periods were expanded from 10-15 periods a week."[65]

As there was a welcoming ceremony for Fourth Principal John Zook (1959-1963), it took no time for him to work with MVS. His wife being a nurse took over all the medical care along with other responsibilities. John Zook started an educational class for teachers to attend and train. He invited teachers from neighboring villages to attend this class. He also looked for an additional dean for the school. When Kim Chang-Soo arrived as the new dean, the educational system at MVS progressed swiftly. Work also continued in all other aspects of the school. For example, new buildings were required and MVS students took action themselves. All the students willingly worked on building the school by constructing the bricks themselves. In addition to the work on the buildings, they worked arduously in the rice fields each year. Under Zook's leadership, the SCM (Student Christian Movement) became more dynamic. When SCM was first created, there were about 90 members, but this number quickly grew to almost all of the boys attending the school. As numbers grew, more activities and departments came about. There were six separate departments:

1. Religious department – helped local churches by

---

[65] Mennonite Central Committee Relief and Educational Missionary Work in Korea1951 to 1971, August 2006, Kim Eel-Sahm and Joanne Voth, p.39.

   supplying Sunday School teachers
  2. Literature department – sponsored essay contests and
   printed Sunday bulletins
  3. Technical department – took pictures
  4. Service department – helping villagers
  5. Physical department – sponsors athletic events
  6. Guidance department – contacted MVS alumni.

These departments led to a time of significant improvement and motivation for the school and the students. A sense of pride became apparent in the students of MVS. The students dined together in the new chapel they built. People from neighboring villages asked for advice on improving crops and livestock. As time passed, progress seemed endless for MVS as more and more people came to help the school. Paul Hochstetler and Harding Duerksen contributed a lot through building roads and even setting up the first telephone system between MVS buildings. Walter and Gladys Rutt arrived and installed a new system for pumping water in the kitchen.

The Fifth Principal, Leland Voth (1963-1967), celebrated MVS's 10th Anniversary Celebration. As Voth was principal, MVS welcomed a new school pastor. His name was Kim Eee-Bong. Kim Eee-Bong not only served as a teacher but also as a counselor for all students and staff at MVS. During this time, international work camps and peace conferences were held. Seeing the success of these events, they spread all throughout Asia bringing about religious reconciliation in many Asian countries such as Korea and Japan. Another huge project Voth undertook was the Extension Program where he tested the nutrient levels in the MVS farms. After the test, he added a fertilizer that increased barley yields by more than 200%! With the advanced farming technology, MVS' crops could withstand typhoons while other farmers' crops could not. MVS came to their aid by giving them technologically advanced crops. The improvements in farming didn't stop there. A newly hired man named Paul Hochstetler further developed dairy facilities. Lee

Young Do, another staff member who received citations and monetary awards, worked diligently using his mechanical ability to drive the Gravely tractor. He also supervised the rice polishing mill.

There wasn't only significant change in agriculture but also a significant change in the spiritual movement in the school. Students from the school traveled to nearby villages to share bible stories and the love of Jesus. They later held classes for villagers after their own classes to learn about the Bible. Under Voth, the school received vocational accreditation. 'MVS is now accredited by the government as a vocational training school. This has been a goal for many years and through much work and red tape was achieved on March 29, 1965. This is when we received the papers from Seoul. This accreditation will help boys who are now in 1st year in high school and classes below to have a government accredited certification at graduation."[66] Another historic event occurred as MVS was connected with the outside world with a telephone system. This gift was made possible by Dr. and Mrs. Isaac Tieszen.

Lee Dong-Keun (1957-1969), the Sixth Principal, came to South Korea from North Korea at 15 to attend school. When he was in college, he wanted to become a teacher in a foreign language but these thoughts changed after working at MVS. After many years of service at MVS he stated that, "My faith in Christ has been enriched and my six years of work at MVS has helped me a lot in gaining many kinds of experience."[67] Due to his faithful work at MVS, he was even sent abroad to study. Following his return from studying abroad, he became the first Korean principal at MVS:

> "Through Lee Dong-Keun's efforts, more than 255 men and women in the Mennonite Community Service Project received institutional training through which they were activated to become better farmers in their

[66] Leland Voth, *MCC Activity Report*, February and March 1965, Mennonite Vocational School, Gyeongsan, Korea
[67] Lee Dong-Keun in letter to MCC 1964

villages and communities. Farmers came to these institutes for 30 days, learning about livestock farming, crop farming, rural sanitation, and daily planning. They were exposed to Christianity and through evening Bible studies, many of them received Christ as their Savior. Besides training these 255 farmers, the MCSP contacted about 1,300 farmers during 1968. During the two years Lee Dong-Keun was director of the school farm, orphanage, hostel and MCSP, staff members learned to take responsibility. They realized that these projects were their own programs geared at helping their own people in the name of Christ."[68]

Even though MVS was changed, its efforts and results during its 20-year history were admirable. By the survey of MVS graduates conducted by Prof. Man-Choon Kang on June 21, 1965, MVS graduates had higher employment and income levels than those from other vocational schools. By Professor Kang's survey, 26.9% of those employed are in clerical type work, compared to 6.3% for KAVA (Korea Association of Voluntary Agencies); 11.5% are in management type work in comparison to KAVA's 7%. This was primarily because many of MVS students had English ability in speaking and writing including technical ability.[69] While 88% of MVS graduates claimed to be leading a religious life, only 72.2% from KAVA claimed it.[70] And 9.5% of MVS and 18.1% of the KAVA groups left their faith after being taught it.

Chung-Suk Chung, a MVS student, demonstrated his vocational school life as follows:

---

[68] Goossen, Henry, *Annual MCC Korea Report 1968* sent to Paul Longacre 11-7-86

[69] Some MVS students participate in a national English speech contest. Two students won second and third prizes on Jun 13, 1959.

[70] *The Recommendation on MVS and Orphans by Kang, Man Choon,* found in the file entitled "MVS Reports 1950-1970," Box 1, File 41, in the "MCC Korean Files, AMC."

"A conversation of my life had come in Mennonite Vocational School. I had an examination to enter Mennonite Vocational Middle School and I passed. It was an agreeable place to me at my first sight. It seemed so peaceful enclosed with small mountains and short pine trees on them and houses and buildings with tiled roofs. In this wonderful place my closed eyes upon the world of Christianity began to open and I found my Shepherd, nay, I was found by Him and given the vision that I could see the path to heaven."[71]

Now many graduates are working as engineers, business managers (including top managers), teachers, pastors, artists, and so on.

2) Christian Child Care Training (CCT)

Christian Child Care Training was MCC's second most popular educational program. The main purpose of the program for training institutional staff was "to improve the day-to-day care of children by increasing the staff's awareness of the children's needs and improving their skills in meeting."[72] When Helen R. Tieszen first traveled to Korea in 1954, she saw a great need for improvement in the training services for child care institutions. This program was planned by MCC in 1962, and started by Helen R. Tieszen in March 1963.[73]

However, Miss Tieszen had previously carried out similar

---

[71] See Chung-Suk Chung, "Story of a Korean Boy," *The Mennonite*, September 25, 1962, pp.621-623.

[72] *The Annual Report of the MCC*, 1962, p.A-27; *MCC Korea 15th Anniversary Brochure*, 1968, p.17; "Korea Child Care Training Program," *The Mennonite*, May 28, 1963, p.363. Helen R. Tieszen's first year in Korea was devoted mainly to the study of the Korean language. This was to get a language ability to communicate adequately with officials, leaders, and children.

[73] Personal communication between SangJin Choi and H.R. Tieszen, December 6, 1996.

programs (1955-1957) when she was seconded to Christian Children's Fund.[74] In 1963, the thirty trainees selected were largely matrons and some housemothers.[75] CCT offered an in-service training course for staffs of child care institutions located in the Gyeongbuk, Gyeongnam, and Pusan areas.[76] Thirty students from various orphanages, sponsored by several agencies, came to study and learn how to take care of children in more meaningful ways.[77] The CCT had two terms in each course that was offered; the first consisted of lectures and demonstrations; the second was the practicum during which time the trainee went back to the orphanage from which she came to carry out assignments given in the first part of the course. Two training courses were usually given in a single year.[78] Many trainees came from different areas of Korea to take the government-accredited program.

MCC sponsored one of the Korean staff members, Miss Chi Dong-Yol to study at Bluffton College and University of Michigan in 1965.[79] Tieszen remarked "Miss Chi my assistant, has been doing a fabulous piece of work both in interpreting and in her contacts with all these people-governmental officials, orphanage superintendents and trainees, as well as children. Without her dedication, we would not function."[80]

According to the report of MCC Korea's 15th Anniversary, by 1968, CCT had completed nine training courses; 202 housemothers and matrons had graduated from the study since the program started in 1963. Even though MCC provided logistical support and the allowance of the program supervisor, operating costs were covered by other agencies. These agencies included World Vision, Christian Children's Fund, Compassion, Catholic Relief Services and the American Korean

---

[74] "Korea Child Care Training Program," *The Mennonite*, May 28, 1963, p.354.
[75] Ibid., p.17.
[76] *The Annual Report of the MCC*, 1963, p.A-19.
[77] Ibid., pp.1-19.
[78] *The Annual Report of the MCC*, 1965, p.A-22; *The Annual Report of the MCC*, 1966, p. A-16.
[79] "Korea Child Care Training Program," 1963, p. 264.
[80] *MCC Korea 15th Anniversary Brochure*, 1968, pp. 17-18.

Foundation.[81]

With the MCC phase-out in Korea, CCT was closed in August 1970. With Helen R. Tieszen as coordinator of this training program for seven and one-half years, 310 mothers and matrons completed their fourteen-week course.[82] Dong-Yol Chi was the first CCT Korean personnel to work with CCT and stayed with the program to the end. Other Korean personnel who provided significant service for a year or more included Young-Hui Joo, Yon-Sook Han, On-Kang Hyun, and In-Sul Lee.[83] Though the program was finished, teachers and graduates experienced the satisfaction of having found an expanse and depth of human understanding across many levels of interpersonal relationships.

3. Economic Self-support

MCC operated several significant projects for economic "self-support"; a sewing project, community service project, and a family-child assistance project.

Although the sewing project started in 1954, the Community Service Project and the Family-Child Assistance Project were planned during the very difficult political situation of the early 1960's. The April Revolution occurred on April 19, 1960. *The MCC Reports and Statistics for 1960* mentioned:

> Korean high school and university students, at the cost of nearly 200 lives and 500 injured, unseated the 12-year-old dictatorial regime of Syngman Rhee and the notorious liberal party. This paved the way for the Second Republic. The elections in July gave the Democratic Party, the former opposition, a strong

---

[81] *The Annual Report of the MCC, 1970*, p.A-11; "Korea Child Care Course 310 Trained in 7 years," 1970, p. 621

[82] *The Annual Report of the MCC*, 1966, p.A-16 and personal communication, H.R. Tieszen, December 6, 1996.

[83] *The Reports and Statistics for 1960*, presented to the MCC, 1961, p.A-14.

majority and a new government. This new government reinstates local autonomy rudely snatched from the people by the controversial National Assembly on December 24, 1958.[84]

On May 16, 1961, a military coup led by General Jung-Hee Park occurred. The military regime emphasized that revolution was necessary to save the country from anarchy and communism. The military government brought about many desirable reforms. However, the economic plight due to political conflicts continued, even though the military government declared a five-year economic development plan. [85] Socio-politically, with extreme poverty and need, widows and orphanages increased. In 1960 widows numbered 549,694, children in orphanages totaled 53,304, compared to 45,260 in 1955, and abandoned children, 2,500.[86] Therefore, in the early 1960s, the Community Service Project and the Family Child Assistance Project for "elf-support" had a very important historical meaning.

1) The Sewing Project

The sewing project was one of the most meaningful economic justice programs based on the biblical foundation: "...The widows, who are in your town, shall come and eat and be satisfied..." (Deut. 14:29).

It was in August 1954 when thirty needy widows were selected by MCC to start a sewing project.[87] These widows were those whose husbands were either killed in battle during the Korean War or who had lost their husbands in other ways. The

---

[84] *The Reports and Statistics for 1961*, 1962, p.A-17.

[85] *The MCC Report of Director Foreign Relief and Services on Asia Commissioner Visit*, September-November, 1961, p.1, Box 1, File 41, in the "MCC Korean Files, AMC."

[86] *MCC Korea 15th Anniversary Brochure*, 1968, p.12.

[87] *The Annual Report of the MCC*, 1953, pp.6-7.

sewing project included a knitting project initiated with American assistance on a large scale through MCC in 1953. "From the start the ladies were taught many different kinds of sewing and some learned knitting, with the completed clothing often being returned to the family or given to needy institutions. The course lasted six months. During that time MCC's sewing instructor was Clara Eschelman followed by Ruth Keim together with their Korean interpreter, Lee Ae Un (Anna) who took over this project after Ruth Keim left. Anna worked there for a total of 6 years until early 1962. In October 1961 she became Mrs. Harry Harms." At that time, a total of $1,601.46 was contributed to the purchase of yarn to be knit up into garments for Korea.[88]

In 1956 MCC equipped the project with 10 sewing machines, 2 knitting machines, a button-hole machine, and a glove knitting machine.[89] However, the purpose of the sewing project was to provide sewing training for widows so that they could support themselves.[90] MCC taught about 12 widows once a year with many different kinds of sewing and knitting machines. MCC provided each with a sewing machine when they graduated. The sewing project was led by four successive instructors until 1968. A total of 158 widow families participated in this program. MCC's sewing machines and training were very helpful for their economic restoration. As one sewing project widow graduate said, "It is now my husband," meaning she had a way to support herself.[91]

2) The Mennonite Community Service Project

The Mennonite Community Service Project (MCSP) became active in December 1960, with emphasis on farming methods improvement.[92] For this project, MCC chose ten villages near Gyeongsan and organized ten 4-H clubs, four women's clubs

---

[88] *The Annual Report of the MCC*, Relief Section, 1956, p.7.
[89] *MCC Korea 15th Anniversary Brochure, p.12*
[90] *The MCC Reports and Statistics for 1968*, Overseas Services, p.A-10.
[91] *The MCC Reports and Statistics for 1961*, p.A-19.
[92] Ibid., p.A-19.

and five farmers' clubs. MCC carried on educational activities in the area of sanitation, health, nutrition and birth control for women, and plant diseases, insect control and the proper use of fertilizers.[93] The early social welfare policies of MCSP included enlarging roads for more convenient farming, building two public bathhouses, building or repairing village meeting halls.[94]

In 1966 a credit union was organized in coordination with the Mennonite Vocational School Credit Union.[95] Local farmers became interested in the MVS livestock loan program in which the recipients returned the firstborn in repayment of the loan. Those who were eligible for such livestock loans were farmers in the ten villages or 4-H members who participated in the extension program.[96] MCC also loaned an earthen block compactor to framers to assist in building church parsonages, barns, and general warehouses.[97] MCSP held a Winter Workshop (or Institute) for farmers and for housewives, providing agricultural leadership in their communities beginning in 1965.[98] In 1967 MCSP held two farmers ̓institutes. During the two-week program, 40 farmers were trained in animal husbandry, crops, rural sanitation and technical farming according to lectures supplied by the Mennonite Vocational School and the Korean government.[99]

A Dairy Farming Institute was started and many different farmers were trained in dairying procedures and animal care. For the ladies, there were a variety of different services including better cooking methods, health training, and family planning practices. The purpose of these services was to make life easier and more rewarding. Through the MCSP program more than 255 men and women received training and approximately 1,300 other farmers received help with counseling during 1968.[100] This

---

93 *MCC Korea 15th Anniversary Brochure*, 1968, p.13.

94 *The MCC Reports and Statistics for 1966*, p.A-15.

95 *MCC Korea 15th Anniversary Brochure*, 1968, p.13.

96 Ibid., p.13.

97 *The MCC Reports and Statistics for 1966*, p.A-15.

98 *The MCC Reports and Statistics for 1967*, p.A-18.

99 *The MCC Reports and Statistics for 1968*, p.A-11.

100 Ibid., p.2.

project, continued from 1960 to 1969, was a long and wide-ranging economic justice program for "self-support" and a community program for realization of Christ's love. Credit union projects, village Bible classes, counseling service banks, and showing educational movies were all well planned programs.

3) Family-Child Assistance Program (FCA)

MCC planned FCA through the analysis of the basic causes of economic poverty as illustrated in <Figure 3>.[101] This analysis suggested that the root causes of poverty were inadequate education, lack of access to resources, and lack of access to capital. The FCA was designed to address these issues through a combination of targeted grants and coordinated interventions.

In 1959 and in the early 1960s, through the natural disaster due to Typhoon Sara of 1959 and the socio-political insecurity due to the April Students Revolution of 1960 and the May 1961 Military coup d'etat, the number of widows and orphans increased rapidly. MCC's FCA program was a suitable policy to alleviate such a problem. FCA, planned in 1962, was an attempt to keep poor families' children in their homes and provide one child per family with an education.[102]

In 1962, seven cases served as a pilot project. [103] MCC provided assistance of $2.50/month for the case families, until they could support themselves.[104] When a Korean social worker was hired in March 1963, this project was expanded as a second family rehabilitation project so that a family could become "self-supporting."

---

[101] *The Report and Statistics for 1962*, p.A-27.
[102] Ibid., p.A-17.
[103] Under the 1962's Korean currency, $2.50 could cover full maintenance including clothing, medicine, school tuition, and books per boy.
[104] This letter is found in the file entitled "Korea FCA Report," BOX 1, File 41, in the "MCC Korean Files, AMC."

<Figure 3>   **Korea Poverty Circle**

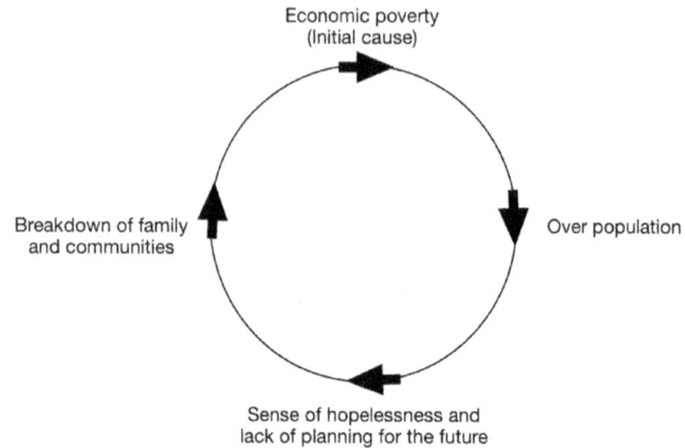

FCA was based on a biblical view of economic justice policy as stated in the following letter *The General Principles and Aims of FCA. This letter* was submitted by Karl Bartsch, MCC Korea Director, on April 5, 1963:

> 1. It will be our aim to maintain and if necessary reunite the family of the client in our program. This will be done by strengthening family ties and remaining together. We are motivated to do this by the Christian concept that the family unit is the basis on which society is built.
> 2. We also aim to give an education to some member of the family who would likely no receive an education unless he received support through this program.
> 3. To implement item one we wish to raise the standard of living of the family we are giving support to and we

aim to make the family unit self-supporting…

4. To facilitate the overall aim to MCC to serve in the name of Christ we aim to provide spiritual guidance where it is needed and requested. We will accept clients regardless of their faith. As well we will be careful not to give the impression to clients that they are "liked better" if they indicate that they are interested in the Christian faith.[105]

In May 1964, two caseworkers assisted 100 client families with $2.50 per month, counsel, and encouragement. In the Shinchon Dong and Shinam Dong areas MCC selected 299 extremely poor households (1,452 persons) and 505 unemployed households (2,565 persons).[106] In 1968, the FCA program had grown to five caseworkers and one full-time supervisor covering a caseload of two hundred families <Table 7>. The number of families in which MCC's economic support was terminated because of their ability to self-support had correspondingly risen to 289 (1,820 persons).[107]

Five hundred and twelve families were helped from 1962 to 1969. Cash assistance was 20,582,850 won ($68,609.50), and material aid was 32,642,270 won ($108,807.50). The breakdown of the total FCA budget for the 1970 fiscal year was $34,068.00; $20,813.40 for FCA sponsorship income for clients (direct support) from MCC, $4364.10 for FCA administration from MCC, and $8,890,50 for MCC administration subsidy.[108]

---

[105] *The Paper for Estimating the Future of FCA Community Development Work*, found in the file entitled "Korea FCA Reports," Box 1, File 41, in the "MCC Korean Files, AMC."

[106] *MCC Korea 15th Anniversary Brochure*, 1985, p.16.

[107] *Korea FCA Budget for 1970 Fiscal Year(1)*, found in the file entitled "Korea FCA Reports," Box 1, File 41, in the "MCC Korean Files, AMC."

[108] *The Korea FCA Report*, May, 1964, pp.3-4, in the "MCC Korean Files, AMC."

<Table 7>   **Source of Referrals for 200 Families**

Referrals	Families	Percentage (%)
Area Office	75	39
Church	52	27
Client Himself	32	16
Community Leader	17	9
Other Agencies	17	9
Total	**200**	**100**

Later, FCA had several outside resources. For example, the Presbyterian Hospital, Daegu, reduced fifty percent all cases referred by caseworkers. In 1964, a machine to make earth-cement blocks was loaned to the FCA program by the American Korean Foundation. Also, government offices provided pamphlets and personnel for education programs and local church pastors helped with spiritual guidance.[109]

According to the data, the original causes of poverty for 200 families were rural exodus (25%), failure in business (20%), hereditary poverty (13%), excessive family medical expenses (12%), death of a householder (10%), etc.[110]

Although the FCA program was terminated on March 31, 1971, with MCC assistance FCA became Daegu Family Welfare, an agency that is still in existence today and provides assistance for needy families with local sponsorship. By 1971, FCA had helped over 655 families to economic independence with 150 of these in the previous 12 months. Seventy percent of FCA terminated cases had been permanently rehabilitated. Thus, we can know that the FCA aim in financial and material assistance based on biblical economic justice – "…but you shall freely open your hand to him, and shall generously lend him sufficient for

---

[109] Ibid., p.16.
[110] Ibid., p.A-12.

his need in whatever he lacks (Deut. 15:8)" – was to encourage economic self-support.

<Table 8>   Length of Assistance Period of 200 Families

Months	Families	Percentage (%)
11 - 13	11	5.5
14 – 16	36	18
17 – 19	122	61
20 – 22	24	12
23 – more	7	3.5
Total	200	100

4. The Healing Mission Project – the Seconded Personnel Program

Promotion of children's health in the post-Korean war period was one of MCC 's concerns. Jacob M. Klassen, former director of MCC Korea, remarked on the necessity of the healing mission for Korean war-orphans and the poor conditions of Korean hospitals as follows:

> With 52 percent of its population under twenty, Korea's problems are just beginning. Some estimate that South Korea has 60,000 orphans. Traditionally Korean widows do not remarry. If they have children, their problem is compounded. By now Korea has quite a few well-organized and well-equipped hospitals…In Korean hospitals there is a considerable gap between theory and practice. Korean nurses are well trained and in good supply…In working side by side with Korean nurses, Mennonite volunteers demonstrated excellent

patient care in actual practice.[111]

Through a cooperative arrangement with the American-Korean Foundation (AKF), nurses from Canada and the U.S. were recruited by MCC and seconded to AKF, which paid their monthly support stipend. Nineteen MCC nurses and two PAX men served in various Korean hospitals from 1954 to 1964 as shown in <Table 9>: Daegu- the Public School Health Program, the Daegu General Hospital, the Daegu Provincial Hospital, and the Daegu Medical College Hospital; Pusan- the Pusan Provincial Health Center, the Australian Presbyterian Hospital, the Pusan Children's Charity Hospital, and the Pusan German Red Cross Hospital; Seoul – the Korea Civil Assistance Command, the Christian Children's Fund, and the Children's Relief Hospital.[112]

These volunteers were sent from U.S. and Canadian Mennonite Churches (MC, GC, MB, and BC), and two of them were sent by the PAX program.[113] Most were nurses who cared for patients and children. They also trained Korean nurses for hospital staff.

In 1954, the second personnel program was started by four nurses on loan to other organizations: Lois Kuhns (the Daegu General Hospital) Katherine Dyck (The Pusan Provincial Health Center), Mrs. J. Harold Yoder (the Taegu Public School Health Program), and Fern Hershberger (the Korea Civil Assistance Command).[114]

---

[111] Jacob M. Klassen, "Korea's Burden," *The Mennonite*, January 23, 1962. pp. 50-52.

[112] See The Annual Report for 1960 and The Annual Report for 1961, Personnel Section.

[113] *The Annual Report for 1954*, Relief Section, p.2

[114] Ibid., p.A-2.

<Table 9>   List of MCC's Medical Personnel (1954-1964)

NO	NAME	ACTIVITY	AGENCY	TERM
1	Mr.s Eva Harsharger* (Korean Civil Assistance Command	MCC Taegu	U/GC/R	/ /53- / /59
2	Pat Yoder* (Taegu Public School Health Program)	MCC Taegu	U/MB/R	/ /53- / /59
3	Katherin Dyck* (Australian Presbyterian. H)	MCC Pusan	C/GC/R	/ /53-10/ /56
4	Lois Kuhns* (Taegu General Hospital)	MCC Taegu	U/OM/R	/ /53-11/15/56
5	Fern Hershberger* (Taejon Provincial Hospital)	MCC Taejon	U/MC/R	/ /54-03/27/57
6	Betty Klippenstein* (Taegu Presbyterian Hospital)	MCC Taegu	Y.NC.R	/ /55-07/08/58
7	Bertha Korneslon* (Children's Charity Hospital)	MCC Pusan	C/MB/R	/ /55-09/28/58
8	Margaret Wiens* (Children's Charity Hospital)	MCC Pusan	C/MB/R	/ /55-09/28/58
9	Twila Brunk* (Children's Charity Hospital)	MCC Taegu	U/MC/R	/ /55-09/28/58
10	Katherine Freisen* (Children's Relief Hospital)	Seoul	U/GC/R	/ /56-09/05/59
11	Arlene Zimmerman* (Children's Charity Hospital)	MCC Pusan	U/MC/R	/ /57-01/27/60
12	Anna Klassen* (Children's Relief Hospital)	Seoul	C/MB/R	/ /57-01/27/60
13	Daniel Roth (Children's Charity Hospital)	MCC Pusan	U/GC/P	/ /58-08/29/61
14	Irma Dyck* (Medical College Hospital)	MCC Taegu	C/GC/R	/ /59-03/07/62
15	Tina Letkeman* (Taegu Presbyterian Hospital)	MCC Taegu	C/GC/R	/ /59-03/07/62
16	Rosemary Zook* (M.V.S.)	MCC Taegu	U/MC/R	/ /59-03/07/62
17	Mabel Brunk* (Children's charity Hospital)	MCC Pusan	U/MC/R	02/10/59-06/ 62
18	Esther Thiessen* (Children's Relief Hospital)	Seoul	C/GC/R	/ /59-07/29/62
19	Dorothy Hoover* (Children's Charity Hospital)	MCC Pusan	C/BC/R	/ /60-03/29/63
20	Lydia Schlabach* (Children Relief Hospital)	Seoul	U/MC/R	/ /60-11/27/63
21	Eugene Dick (Children's Charity Hospital)	MCC Pusan	U/GC/P	/ /61-12/02/64

*-Nurse   R-Relief   P-Pax

At Pusan Children's Charity Hospital (PCCH) MCC PAX man, Eugene Dick, acted as assistant to the Korean superintendent and provided liaison with western personnel for the hospital. [115] Called "nurse advisors," the MCC nurses at PCCH worked closely with the Korean director of nurses and the entire nursing staff. MCC nurses helped teach and model the care of ill children in the hospital. PCCH staff nurses attended classes occasionally. Later, a longer course was planned to give graduate nurses better preparation in theory and practice in areas of growth and development, health maintenance, and pediatric nursing. In planning for instruction for them.[116]

Another task was liaison with the local Armed Forces Hospital. Extra supplies were often donated. Out-dated vaccines, drugs, samples, and materials that could be recycled were obtained. Recalling when an army orthopedist visited PCCH and assisted with surgery, Mabel V. Brunk remarked "MCC personnel helped turn swords into plowshares."

5. Evaluation of the MCC's Policy

As I emphasized in the main section, MCC's policy was a "messianic peace mission" based on biblical concern for helping alienated, orphaned, and widowed. It was a cooperative program between all of the Mennonite denominations and both countries' governments (U.S. and Canada). MCC shipped 19,886,000 pounds of supplies to South Korea during a twenty-year period. Andrew Leatherman, former MCC PAX man, recalled his life in Korea:

> "...I took to sitting cross-legged-Oriental style- on the floor in a Korean church...I found a real Christian welcome at the little church I adapted. The brief bows, handshakes, or nods or many increasingly familiar faces

---

[115] In case of PCCH, student nurses from Pusan National University Hospital came for periods of experience caring for infants and children.
[116] Out of 19,886,000 pounds of supplies, 14,548,000 represented United States food for peace commodities and 522,000 pounds, Canada government food commodities. See *The Reports and Statistics for 1971*, p.A-13.

> each Sunday were warm and friendly…For me to attend
> a poor Korean church has taken courage. It has meant
> cramps, freezing toes in midwinter, when there's no
> heat…This has been an opportunity to grow more
> broadly and deeply in my Christian life, and a chance
> for the Spirit of God to more openly with me."[117]

MCC's workers devoted themselves to planting truth, justice, and love with joy in the poor country, Korea.[118] During the twenty-year period, 77 MCC overseas workers served in South Korea. Out of 77 workers, 21 were PAX workers, and 56 persons were relief workers. Nineteen nurses and two PAX men worked in hospitals during the period. Out of the 77 workers, 64 were U.S. MCC workers, and 13 were Canadian MCC workers. They were supported by Mennonite denominations as shown in <Table 10>.

In his book entitled, *The Preferential Option: A Christian and Neoliberal Strategy for Latin America's Poor,* Army L. Sherman defined "holistic development" as a multifaceted concept including the economic, the political, the social, and the moral-cultural. His notion also implied a Christian conception of public order. He believed "Christian NGO's both out of their responsibilities as disciples and out of their commitment to economic advancement, have a role to play in the cultural component of development work."[119] Similarly, MCC's policy was a holistic peace mission based on the components of material aid, economic self-support, academic education and training, social service, and spiritual education.

---

[117] See Andrew Leatherman, "Korean Church Cramps," *The Mennonite,* February 16, 1971, p.111.

[118] *The Reports and Statistics for 1971,* p.A-13.

[119] Army L. Sherman, *Preferential Option: A Christian and Neoliberal Strategy for Latin America's Poor,* Grand Rapids, Michigan: William B. Eerdmans Publishing Company, 1992, pp.36-40.

<Table 10>   MCC-Korea Workers' Nationalities and Denominations

Agency	United States	Canada	Total
MC	36	1	37
GC	21	4	25
MB	1	7	8
LC	4	.	4
BC	.	1	1
EMB	1	.	1
Total	63	13	76

MCC's two important economic self-supporting projects were the Sewing Project to provide sewing training for widows so that they could learn to wholly support themselves and their families,[120] and the Family Child Assistance Program to raise funds to encourage family solidarity and independence. Therefore, MCC's most significant resources for Korean families' economic self-support were funds, technology, and facilities.

MCC's two important educational programs were Mennonite Vocational School (MVS) and the Christian Child Care Training (CCT). MVS was designed to give war-orphaned boys vocational education, and CCT's intent was to train leaders to educate orphans and poor children. In addition, MCC personnel led English Bible studies to nurture spiritual life among orphans and village people. Therefore, MCC's educational policies were based on the harmonization of self-support training, education, and spirituality.

It was difficult for MCC to plan a socio-economic mission policy in the politically and economically unstable situation of Korea. Even though there are several difficulties, they still overcame their obstacles.

First, under the unstable political situation in Korea, it was

---

[120] *Korea MCC 15th Anniversary Brochure*, 1968, p. 12.

hard to get a long-term mission. Therefore, most MCC workers were short-term. Out of 77 workers, 58 were temporary -term workers (one-three years), 10 mid-term workers (four years), and 9 long-term workers (five years and more). Short-term personnel included 11 were one-year workers, and 47 were three-year workers. Only four worked for more than five years which is less than 10% of the total workers. Even though many short-term workers did not have time to learn Korean, they overcame language barriers well. They also taught English to Korean staff and volunteers. They could easily help Mennonite workers realize their Korea program. However, for the long - term workers, MCC provides time and money for the formal language instruction of its workers. They were enrolled in a three- or six-month Korean language study course at Yonsei University in Seoul. Workers Helen R. Tieszen, and Lee and Jody Voth studied at Yonsei University for a year.

Secondly, the unstable Korean education system made it difficult for them to get approval for MVS as a technical high school. Korean local government did not understand about the formal school for all war orphans. At the time, the Korean government did not have any facilities for school-level orphanages. The government also had no qualified teachers to teach war orphans at school-level. The government, however, could not decide easily to approve MCC. Since the Korean Civil War, many orphanages have been built. The Korean Orphanage Association was also organized at this time. These orphanages needed support from the government both materially and financially. The Korean government recognized that if MCC was given accreditation other orphanages would raise complaints. Fortunately, the Korean government understood MCC's staff and program would be enough to manage the schools of orphanages. MCC's plan focused on technical high schools and mid-level high schools for the Korean War orphans. In terms of education for economic self-dependence, it was a very creative project.

Thirdly, that MCC withdrew their program after 24 years of work also was not easy for them to decide. The fact that other organizations that worked with MCC during the same period continue to work today (e.g., World Vision, Holt Children Center...). MCC decided that Korea had rapid economic development, so they did not need to stay in Korea continuously. So, MCC relocated Korean workers to Africa and the Middle East to help and aid. However, I think MCC needs to start a second mission, not only material aid rather than a peacebuilding program in Korea.

Lastly, we can think about MCC's church planting; is it necessary or not? MCC's Korea project focused on community development more than church planting. The split of the Korean Presbyterian Church occurred in a serious way.[121] MCC did not wish to establish another denomination in Korea as a result of this. However even though MCC emphasized that MCC was not a mission organization, but a relief/service organization, they can plant churches.[122]

By the report of MVS conference held on December 1962 at MVS, students requested to build their church up, opening it more to villages. They also requested to have evangelists who help in churches in ten villages and teach Sunday school. About 150 small children from neighboring villages attend Sunday school every Sunday morning at MVS. It was an excellent opportunity to think about the necessity of church planting based on Mennonite tradition and faith. According to the *Diary of Asia Trip* by Robert W. Miller, the two most respectable and largest Presbyterian Church congregations also emphasized the necessity of a Mennonite church in Korea, positively. Miller

---

[121] See *The Report of the MCC*, 1959, Section A, p.S-8:

> "The Christian church is beset with some rather serious problems. In the Presbyterian church, for example, a split has occurred between the members of the Assembly 54 with the result that there are now two Presbyterian churches. Missionaries and other Christian workers are trying to bring about a settlement between the two factions."

[122] *The Reports and Statistics for 1960*, p.A-14; See *the Reports on the Kyong San MVS for Orphan Boys* submitted to the United Nations Women's Guild, May, 1955 and The Asia Foundation, January, 1956, in the "MCC Korean Files, AMC."

wrote of his interview with Dr. Lee Sang-Kuen (pastor of the largest Presbyterian congregation in Daegu) as follows:

> He said the Mennonite work in the Daegu area is respected. However, if we leave now, we would likely be forgotten because we do not have a Mennonite church. He encouraged us to consider starting a congregation in Daegu and concentrating on special services to the Korean church. He felt we might help with the Korean revival program being planned, become involved in student work, and in literature production.[123]

Miller also reported on his interview with Dr. Han Kyung-Jik (pastor of the largest Presbyterian congregation in Seoul) as follows:

> He feels there is still a great opportunity to reach people with the Christian message. He would welcome more groups to work in Korea. He feels colleges would welcome foreign English teachers, and students could be invited to evening Bible classes. He also pointed out the need for work in rural areas.[124]

These two Korean pastors' comments about the necessity of a Mennonite mission in Korea were very prophetic. They were like McGavran's question in *Decisions in Mission Today*, "Withdrawing Missionaries- Right or Wrong?"[125]

If MCC taught the Mennonites' historical faith tradition of martyrdom, the Korean church could find a contact-point with the Mennonites. With the spirit of martyrdom, the Korean church battled against Japanese imperialism, communism, and

---

[123] Robert W. Miler, *Diary of Asia Trip*, submitted to MCC, 1965, p.6.
[124] Ibid., p.8
[125] Donald A. McGavran, *Momentous Decisions in Missions Today*, Grand Rapids: Baker Book House, 1984, pp. 191-200.

the military regime's autocracy over 210 years in Catholicism and 110 years in Protestantism. Even though we have a short history of Christian persecution, thousands of church leaders and laymen, and hundreds of foreign missionaries died. Through the Korean Civil War, the Korean church suffered materially, but its faith was rich. Since the 1970s when MCC withdrew from Korea, the Korean church has had distinguished growth through prayer meetings filled with the Holy Spirit. In addition, it has had revival meetings using Bible studies. Mennonites also have a long martyrdom history lodged in their Anabaptist roots. Mennonites were persecuted at the January 21, 1525 meeting. This would lead to social difficulties if left unchecked.[126] The history of Mennonite until the mid-seventeenth century when they planted their faith in North America, like the Puritans was a Christian martyr history.[127]

In addition, MCC's economic relief policy towards South Korea since the Korean War was based on the messianic peace mission. Nobody can deny the fact that MCC's workers play a significant role in the socio-economic self-support of the Korean people. In modern society Korea also needs a life-evangelical based church like the Mennonite. Mennonite Churches will help Korean churches, which want a Messianic peace community vision.

Conclusion:
The Necessity of the Second Mission

The MCC's closing period in Korea began in 1965 – the withdrawal of the healing mission project (the Second Personnel project) and the signature of the Japan-Korean Normalization

---

126 Cornelius J. Dyck, ed., *An Introduction to Mennonite History*, Second Edition, PA, Herald Press, 1981, pp.50-61.
127 Ibid., p.188.

Treaty for economic development.

According to some interview with former Korea MCC directors, the main reasons for the withdrawal were the burden of economic support, a necessity of relief for other countries (especially in Africa), and Korea's economic development for self-support. However, while MCC worked in Korea for twenty years (1950-1971), the historical material aid of Mennonites in Korea was neglected. Their historical dedication and sacrifice are preserved in the archives of the Mennonite Church at Goshen College, in Goshen, Indiana. Korea has had no Mennonite organizations or Mennonite persons for twenty-four years (1971-1995): this rich history has been forgotten by the Korean people.

From the MVS graduates and Mennonite Oriented Koreans the necessity of starting a Mennonite church in Korea, they have emphasized. The most effective way to make up for it is to plant Mennonite faith in martyrdom and peace in the modern Korean context. Fortunately, in 1996 the Mennonite Church reestablished one worker family to support the Abba Shalom Community towards the building of the Korean Anabaptist center. My hope is that this presence will grow into a greater and more effective commitment to Mennonite mission in Korea. In addition, I would like to emphasize that the slogan for the second mission policy should be "Messianic Shalom Mission" as it relates to the current Korean socio-political situation.

The former missionaries as living witnesses are very helpful for the second Korea mission. First of all, MCC must activate a Reunion Meeting of the former Korea missionaries, and plan a strategy program for the new Korea mission. MCC also must organize a meeting of Korean people who are associated with MCC during Mennonite mission work in Korea. Finally, MCC must give Koreans the opportunity to learn about the Mennonites and their peace movement.

Therefore, it is very worthwhile for MCC to plan a meeting, seminar and conference harmonized with MCC, former missionaries, and Korean people who are oriented to or interested in the Mennonite way of faith. I will touch on more specific suggestions in chapter 4.

3

MCC's RECONCILIATION PROGRA IN SOUTH KOREA

Introduction

Korean political situation of 1964-1965, led by President Park Jung-Hee, seemed stable externally. After the Japan-Korea Normalization Treaty was signed, the inner political situation entered a new phase due to students' and opposition parties' vigorous demonstrations and petitions. The government's main policy toward Japan was driven by economic considerations. Therefore, the government signed a rapprochement with Japan to get indemnity, despite Korea's legitimate grievances and disturbing student riots.[128]

However, beginning in 1964 a reconciliation movement between Korean and Japanese churches was begun interdenominationally, without a political aim. MCC had a commendable goal of reconciliation between Christian leaders and youth. MCC's peace efforts included an International Peace Conference and International Reconciliation Work Camps. With a study of the historical backgrounds of the conflict between Koreans and Japanese, I would like to arrange and evaluate MCC 's reconciliation policy between 1963 and 1970.

Historical Backgrounds of the Conflict between the Koreans and the Japanese

The Early Japanese Invasion of Korea (1592-1597)

---

[128] *The Reports and Statistics for 1964,* 1965, p. A-23, presented to the MCC meeting in annual session at the Hotel Atlantic, Chicago, Illinois, January 15 and 16, 1965.

The first significant conflict between Korea and Japan took place when Japan invaded Korea in the latter part of the 16th century. Toyotomi Hideyoshi, the Japanese general who established his hegemony in Japan, attacked China to force the Chinese to recognize him as the true master of Japan. Although Toyotomi requested the Korean government to allow the passage of Japanese troops through Korea, the government denied his request. This is because Korea was a vassal to China which refused an alliance with Japan. At last, 160,000 Japanese with modern weapons invaded Korea twice, in 1592 and in 1597. Korean troops armed with swords could not defend their government against Japanese troops with rifles. Seoul, Korea's capital, fell within two weeks of the invasion. King Sonjo and his court had to leave Seoul for Uiju.[129] The Japanese troops then advanced north as Pyongyang and Hamheung to complete the country's subjugation.

Through peace negotiations with the Chinese, Hideyoshi proposed the division of Korea—the north was to be a self-governing China satellite, and the south was to remain in Japanese hands.[130] However, these talks failed, and Hideyoshi launched a second invasion in 1597. In this invasion the Japanese troops failed because of the Korean troops' strong defense and Hideyoshi's death (1598). Despite Japanese troops withdrawing, numerous Korean commoners were carried off as prisoners. Moreover, thousands were slaughtered and farmlands (especially in Gyeongsang province) were devastated. The effects of the war included serious economic instability including famine and diseases. Although Korea-Japan relations were restored partly during the 1600's, the Korean people described Japanese brutality in writing and preserved it in their minds.

---

[129] Han Woo-Keun, *The History of Korea*, Trans. By Lee Kyung-Shik, Ed. By Grafton K. Mintz, Honolulu:East-West Center Press, 1971, p.271.
[130] Andrew C. Nahm, *Korea: Tradition & Transformation-A History of the Korean People*, Seoul:Hollym, 1988, p.24

Japanese Colonial Rule (1910-1945)

Japan's enforcement of an unequal treaty with Korea was the first in Korea's subjection as a Japanese colony.[131] When Western countries, as well as China, made advances towards Korea through diplomatic channels, the new Meiji government of Japan requested the establishment of new diplomatic and commercial relations with Korea. On September 22, 1875, Japanese troops landed on Kanghwa Island and attacked Ch'ojijin, killing 33 and wounding 16 Korean soldiers. On February 26, 1876, Japan concluded an amity and commerce agreement with Korea at Kanghwa through gunboat diplomacy. In order to eliminate Chinese influence from Korea, Japan declared war on China on August 1, 1894. During that time, the Korean government was persuaded to sign a treaty alliance with Japan. During the Russo-Japanese war (1904-1905), Japan forced the Korean government to sign a protocol which included advice from Japan regarding improvements in administration.

Japanese policy of annexation of Korea was promoted by help of the United States and the decisions made at the Russo-Japanese Peace Conference at Portsmouth, New Hampshire. In July, 1905, the Taft-Katsura Agreement was signed by the Japanese Prime Minister, Katsura Taro, and the American Secretary of War. In this agreement, the United States recognized "Japan's interests in Korea in return for a Japanese promise not to interfere or raise objections to American rule in the Philippines."[132] At the Russo-Japanese Peace Conference, Russia also officially recognized Korea as a Japanese protectorate. Due to Japan's forceful intervention in 1907, the Korean government was deprived of its right to control its own political and legal affairs.

On August 22, 1910 Japan officially annexed Korea. Korea was subject to Japanese colonialism for 36 years, until World War

---

131   Chung Kyung-Cho, *Korea Tomorrow: Land of the Morning Calm*, New York:Macmillan Company, 1956, p.165.
132 Han Woo-Keun, *The History of Korea*, p.447.

II. In the colonial period, the Korean government lost all its sovereignty, including its political, economic, cultural, and religious rights. Leaders of anti-Japanese and nationalistic movements were arrested. Japan banned Korean newspapers and magazines, along with the Korean language. A number of Koreans lost their land, and Japanese companies took over trade, mining, fisheries, and manufacturing industries.

Japan planned numerous programs to assimilate Koreans into Japanese culture and ideologies. They made it compulsory to change Korean names into Japanese names. College students were recruited into the Japanese imperial army and died at war. Many young women were sent to be 'comfort women' for Japanese soldiers; many died in the war. Japan's inhumane activity in Korea during this period of colonial rule has caused the most serious antagonism towards Japan in Korean minds until the present.

Despite the wild demonstrations, President Park sent Kim Chong-P'il to Tokyo to negotiate with the Japanese for a normalization treaty. When the students found out about Kim's visit, the demonstrations climaxed; the students screamed insults at the Japanese government and even demanded President Park's resignation. June 3 saw the Korean government declare martial law in Seoul until July 26.

The normalization treaty with Japan was signed on December 18, 1965. Japan's payment of a $300 million indemnity to South Korea helped the Korean government implement the new five-year economic development plan begun in 1967. In spite of this, the imbalance in trade with Japan continued as well as the antagonistic feeling toward it.

MCC's Efforts for Reconciliation

1) Ferd Ediger's Efforts
A "people-to-people" reconciliation program between Korea

and Japan was suggested by Ferd Ediger, a peace worker from MCC Japan in 1963. The first reconciliation plan was a work camp for reconciliation between MCC Korea and MCC Japan. Ediger discussed a reconciliation work camp for young Christians with Karl Bartsch, MCC Korea director. In 1964 Ediger mentioned an inter-church fellowship and dialogue between Korea and Japan through his letter to Karl Bartsch as follows:

> As last year, I come to you again by letter to ask whether you might be in a position this year to have a work camp of some natures that you would give some of our Japanese brethren an opportunity to have some fellowship and dialogue with Korean Christians as well as helping them some project that takes the form of work.... I noticed that last year you were new in Korea and am wondering whether you would now be ready to invite some of our energetic Young People to help you.[133]

Bartsch also shows his positive reaction to Ediger's project through his letter to Ediger on May 1, 1964. Bartsch mentioned that he had written to Wilbert Shenk who had visited Korea as an MCC Commissioner from February 10th to 16th, to ask his support for the reconciliation project as follows:

> I think it is food for Japanese and Korean Christians to establish a dialogue of some sort. Out here we are very much aware that this is sadly lacking.... Most of all I would be interested in working out something to increase better relations between Korean Christians and Japanese Christians. It might interest you to know that today I wrote to Wilbert Shenk, asking his support for

---

[133] *Ferd Ediger's Letter to Karl Bartsch*, April 16, 1964, found in the file entitled "Japan-Korea Relations," Box1, File 41, in the "MCC Korean Files, AMC."

a project that is opening up.[134]

In 1964, Ferd arranged two Christian Student Peace Seminars in the Kyushu and Tokyo areas. These seminars planned by Ediger and Carl Beck, MCC Japan peace workers, became a cornerstone of the reconciliation program between Korea and Japan (see next chapter). He also participated in the activities of the Anti-Hydrogen Bomb Movement: Gensuikyo-Japan Council Against Atomic and Hydrogen Bombs, Gensuikin-sponsored by the Japan Socialist Party and the Sohyo Labor Union, and the Kakkin Kauigi-National Convention Against Atomic Bombs and for Construction of Peace.[135]

2) Carl Beck's Efforts

The role of Rev. The Mennonite Board of Mission (Elkhart) peace worker, Carl Beck, played a very significant role in this specialized ministry.137 His peace work, as a successor to Ferd Ediger, was launched on July 1, 1964. He had already engaged in some peace seminars in Japan; the Fifth Missionary Seminar was themed "Communicating the Gospel in Japan." It was convened in Hayama, January 6-9, 1964. The first free church seminar was held April 28-29 in Osaka. Two seminars for university students were held in 1964; one in Miyazaki, Kyushu (May 3-5), and the other in Tokyo (May 8-10). Carl Beck participated as an advisor to a committee that met monthly in preparation for the next seminar. Besides the Hayama and Christian student seminars, he met monthly with a group of Protestant, Catholic, and Orthodox seminary personnel to discuss differences and explore areas of reconciliation.[136]

---

[134] *Karl Barsch's Letter to Ferd Ediger*, May 1, 1964, found in the file entitled "Japan-Korea Relations," Box1, File 41, in the "MCC Korean Files, AMC."

[135] Carl Beck, *Japan Mennonite Peace Mission*, Quarterly Report, July 1 to September 30, 1964, pp. 1-2 founded in the file entitled "Japan-Korea Relations," Box 1, File 41, in the "MCC Korean Files, AMC."

[136] *The Reports and Statistics for 1965*, 1966, p.B-5.

In 1965, three Christian University Student Peace Conferences planned by Carl Beck were held in Tokyo, Miyazaki and Osaka. The theme of the Tokyo peace seminar April 1 through 4 was "Reconciliation in East Asia." The seminar became a cornerstone of Korea-Japan relationships. Mr. Lee Un-Shik, a representative of MCC Korea and three Japanese-born Korean students participated in the seminar.[137] In this seminar some Japanese-born Korean students mentioned Korean-Japanese: "Third-generation people cannot even get foreign resident status, and first and second-generation still can never become Japanese citizens, even though both countries signed the normalization treaty."[138]

Carl Beck introduced a theology of peace and reconciliation by arranging three reconciliation work camps and two international peace seminars in Taegu and Tokyo, from 1965 to 1967.

3) Fumio Kurita's Efforts

The elimination of the antagonism between Korea and Japan formed by Japan's invasion was a very serious issue for MCC Japan. One man decided to do something. He was Fumio Kurita, a young evangelist of the Osaka Mennonite Brethren Church.[139] Kurita recognized the antagonism between Korea and Japan well because he "had grown up near a Korean settlement in Osaka, and one of his best friends was a Korean."[140] He knew that Koreans who lived in Japan "had little hope of ever advancing beyond the very lowest of day laborers."[141] He also recognized a historical conflict that was formed by Japan's invasions : "It was after the war, while I was in Bible school, that I learned what we Japanese had done to the Koreans. It made me ill for several days. Now I know "why my Korean friends and

---

[137] *The Reports and Statistics for 1964*, 1965, p.B-5.
[138] Carl Beck, "Peace Witness Is Mission," *Gospel Herald*, June 1, 1965.
[139] Carl Beck, "Trek to Korea," *The Mennonite*, November 2, 1965.
[140] Loc. cit.
[141] Loc. cit.

I drifted apart."[142] Kurita recognized that both countries needed reconciliation in Christ:

> I have the strong conviction that we, as Japanese Christians, should show our love in Christ toward Korean Christians by asking their forgiveness for what we did to them in our past years, so that we might be reconciled in Christ, and the peace of the Lord, who is the Prince of Peace, might be created among us…. Such reconciliation is ours through Christ. It is a gift. We need nothing but accept it. We must learn from our Korean brethren to pray, to witness, to give, and to forgive.[143]

Kurita's first visit to Korea in November, 1964 was the start of the reconciliation between two nationalities among whom Mennonites served.[144] As a first-step towards reconciliation, he suggested that his Mennonite Brethren Church invite a Korean MCC caseworker to Japan.[145] In 1965, Lee Un-Shik, a social worker in the Korean MCC program, spent nearly six weeks in Japan visiting Mennonite churches and participating in two of the student peace seminars. Kurita also co-worked with Carl Beck's peace program in Japan. He performed well as a seminar leader by providing a spiritually warm setting for the Student Christian Peace Seminar in Osaka.[146]

MCC's Policy of the Reconciliation

---

[142] Loc. cit.

[143] Ibid., p.679.

[144] *The Reports and Statistics for 1964*, p.A-24; *The Reports and Statistics for 1965*, p.B-4.

[145] *The Reports and Statistics for 1964*, p. A-23.

[146] Carl Beck, "Students Discuss Peace," *Gospel Herald*, September 7, 1965.

The First Reconciliation Work Camp in Taegu, Korea

The first MCC international work camp in Korea was held at the Gyeong San vocational school in 1954 to build a second boy's dormitory. Robert Lee organized and directed the camp. The foreign participants, besides Robert Lee, included four PAX men, Valentine Yutzy, Woodrow Ramseyer, Howard Burkholder and Harry Harms, and a mixed team of four from the Hollywood Presbyterian Church in the USA.[147] The second international work camp was organized next summer at the edge of the camp at Kyung Pook National University to build a student center. Besides Robert Lee and the four PAX men the camp had two participants from the Philippines and one American missionary from Japan.[148] The third international work camp held in Daegu was led by Valentine Yutzy.[149] However, the first "people-to-people" reconciliation program between Korea and Japan which had already been suggested by Ferd Ediger since 1963 was a work camp to provide a forum for fellowship and dialogue as well as a concrete project.

Carl Beck and Karl Bartsch, Korea MCC director, planned the first reconciliation work camp in July,1964, in which Japanese Christian young people came to Korea to help in the building program at the Mennonite Vocational School.[150] Beck planned an educational program of cultural understanding of Korean for the Japanese youth including Korean life, industry, farming, fishing, and the church in Korea.[151] Through the ten days of the program between July 23 and August 2, 1965, they realized the miracle of reconciliation which had happened among them: "The animosities and atrocities of sixty years of

---

[147] Personal communication, Robert Lee, November 14, 1996.
[148] Loc. cit.
[149] Loc. cit.
[150] *Leland Voth's Letter to Carl Beck*, August 26, 1965, found in the file entitled "Japan-Korea Relations," Box 1, File 41, in the MCC Korean Files, AMC."
[151] *The Diary of Robert W. Miller's Asia Trip*, MCC, Akron, Pennsylvania, March 20-May 1, 1965, p.2.

Japanese occupation had built barriers of fear and hate."[152] Japanese youth apologized for the Japanese colonial rule and Korean youth forgave them in Christ Jesus who broke down the dividing wall.

The work camp brought together thirteen Koreans, ten representatives of the Japanese Mennonite churches including one woman, and one North American young woman.[153] Participants in the work camp terraced a hillside, working approximately ten days, as well as visiting Korean cultural sites and discussing issues of reconciliation between Korea and Japan.[154] Beck emphasized the significance of this first work camp as follows:

This experiment in reconciliation was especially significant in that twenty years after the Japanese expulsion from Korea, the churches of the two countries still have practically no contact with each other. Even in Japan, where Korean churches and Japanese churches are in the same area in Osaka or Tokyo, there is no inter-church fellowship. Repeatedly the Korean church has expressed its desire for reconciliation.[155]

The Second and Third Reconciliation Work Camp

The second reconciliation work camp was held in Tokyo in July 1966. Participants of the work camp were predominantly

---

[152] *Carl Beck's Letter to Lyle Troyer*, July 10, 1965, found in the file entitled "Japan-Korea Relations," Box 1, File 41, in the "MCC Korean Files, AMC."

[153] Carl Beck, "Korea Workcamp Wins Japanese Friends," *The Mennonite*, September 28, 1965.

[154] *The Reports and Statistics for 1965*, p. B-4. Ten representatives of the Japanese Mennonite churches were Yuzo Moritani, Jiro Sakai, Terumi Tamaki (female), Hideo Morita, Masaru Oyama, Hideaki Tukada, Hisashi Kagyo, Hajime Kaneshige, Shozo Sato, and Ukichi Kondo. See *Carl Beck's Letter to Lyle Troyer*, July 10, 1965.

[155] *Karl Bartsch's Letter to Whom This May Concern*, July 6, 1965, found in the file entitled "Japan-Korea Relations" Box 1, File 41, in the "MCC Korean Files, AMC."

Mennonite youth, but did not exclude others.[156] The work camp brought together eleven Korean representatives, nineteen Japanese, and five North Americans. One North American participant described this work camp as follows: "For 30 years I have been active in church camp programs in America. Never in all my experience have I seen the Holy Spirit so evidently at work in young people's hearts and lives. I shall never forget this."[157]

Originally Korea and Japan MCC planned to hold the third reconciliation Work Camp on July 13 to 25, 1967, with the following purpose: "(1) To effect reconciliation between Christians of Japan and Korea, (2) To increase good will between the youth of the two countries, (3) To be of real service to the country of Korea through work projects, and (4) To make amends to the people of Korea for their suffering during the Japanese occupation."[158] The date was changed to July 21-August 1 and was held at Wolsong Hope Village, near Gyeongju city,[159] in order to join with the 10th international work camp sponsored by the Korea work camp conference with the help of the Ministry of Health and Social Affairs, the Republic of Korea.[160] This camp's aim was to provide an opportunity for young people to do voluntary service, living together not only for labor itself, but for the fellowship and cooperation between campers and community.[161] The Third Work Camp's project was "to level a wooded hillside on the compound of the Ai Rak Won Leprosarium, an American Leprosy Mission Hospital, and to lay

---

[156] Carl Beck, "Korea Workcamp Wins Japanese Friends."

[157] *The Reports and Statistics for 1966*, 1967, p.B-5.

[158] "Korea-Japan Reconciliation," *The Canadian Mennonite*, Tuesday, November 1, 1966, p.1.

[159] *Henry W. Goossen's Letter of Invitation and Guarantee*, April 27, 1967, found in the file entitled "Japan-Korea Relations," Box 1, File 41, in the "MCC Korean Files, AMC."

[160] *Henry W. Goossen's Letter of Invitation and Guarantee*, May 1, 1967.

[161] *The Reports of the International Work Camp in Korea*, Korea Work Camp Conference, 1967, found in the file entitled "Japan-Korea Relations," Box 2, file 41, in the "MCC Korean Files, AMC."

the foundation for a large new rehabilitation center.[162] Thirteen Japanese, eighteen Korean, Two Taiwanese, and seven Americans from Japan participated in the joint work camp.[163]

The final work camp before MCC's termination in Korea was the Asian Reconciliation Work Camp organized by Carl Beck in August 1970. This work camp brought 25 campers from Korea, Japan, Taiwan, Indonesia and India for two weeks in Hong Kong.[164] However, the Asian youth reconciliation work camps were continued sporadically outside of Korea by the Asia Mennonite Conference into the late 1980's. The Asia Mennonite Conference also sponsored a return work camp for the 20th anniversary of the first work camp in Korea in 1985.

All the work camps organized by MCC in Asia played a key role in reconciliation among other Asian churches. In addition, they resolved conflict resolution between the Japanese and the Korean church.

The First International Peace Conference in Daegu, Korea (1965)

The first peace conference for reconciliation between the Korean church and the Japanese church was held at the Mennonite Vocational School, Daegu on October 28-29, 1965.[165] The MCC Korea conference planning committee was made up of 15 members representing various religious groups in the Daegu area; three Presbyterian groups, Methodist,

---

[162] *Korea Work Camp Conference Director's Letter to Dear Sirs,* June 1, 1967, found in the file entitled "Japan-Korea Relations," Box 1, File 41, in the "MCC Korean Files, AMC."

[163] Carl Beck, "Surprised by Forgiveness Japanese Meet Koreans," *The Mennonite,* October 24, 1967.

[164] Loc. cit. By *Henry W. Goossen's Letter to Ministry of Justice Republic of Korea,* July 4, 1967, eleven of 13 Japanese were Ito Heihachiro, Inamine Yoshira, Morita Michko, Morita Hiroko, Yamamoto Akiko, Kagyo Hisashi, Arita Chisako, Takanori Sasaki, Kobayashi Akihiko, Sekinaga Mitsuhiko, and Yoshida Michiko.

[165] *The Reports and Statistics for 1970,* 1971, p.B-3.

Holiness, Salvation Army, YMCA and YWCA, and MCC in Korea.[166] They planned a seminar on the theme "Reconciliation, a Gift from God."

In the opening worship service of this seminar, Carl Beck spoke about the theme. Other topics were "The Theological Aspects in Reconciliation" (Chul-Soo Yoon, pastor of Suh Myun Church), "The Ethical Viewpoints in Reconciliation" (Kwang-Hoon Kim, chaplain of Dong San Presbyterian Hospital), "Reconciliation in Labor and Management" (Jae-Jin Kim, professor of Kyung Pook University), "Reconciliation of Old and Young Generations" (Sung Hyuk Kim, professor of Kyung Pook National University [167] and "Reconciliation in International Aspect" given by Chang-Woo Rhee, professor of Taegu College and Reiji Oyama, pastor of a church in Tokyo. Dr. Sang-Keun Lee, pastor of First Presbyterian Church in Taegu moderated open discussion.[168] Especially Kwang-Hoon Kim declared: "Reconciliation is the object of Christian faith…. Faith, charity, and hope can be certain only (as they) accomplish the work of reconciliation." Dr. Chang Woo-Rhee also declared "There must be a great deal of sincerity and understanding (on the part of) both Korea and Japan to solve the difficult relationships of the two countries, (left as an aftermath) of a long colonial rule. We must all face up squarely to our past

---

[166] *The Reports and Statistics for 1965*, p. B-4 *Brochure of the Program for Reconciliation Seminar*, October 28-29, 1965, found in the file entitled "Japan-Korea Relations," Box 1, File 41, in the "MCC Korean Files, AMC."

[167] *The Reports and Statistics for 1965*, p.4-5; *Leland Voth's letter to Planning Committee*, August 26, 1965, found in the file entitled "Japan-Korea Relations," Box 1 File 41, in the "MCC Korean Files, AMC."

[168] In his presented paper he argued the problem of the Korean family system: "The traditional Korean family system is parent-centered…It is difficult for the newly married couple to live separately from their parents, and the lack of a social security system for the aged in our society makes the problem of supporting parents more complicated." See the paper of "Re-evaluation of the Korean Family System" presented by Kim, Sung Hyuk, found in the file entitled "Japan-Korea Relations," Box 1, File 41, in the "MCC Korean Files, AMC."

history before we can face the future as brothers." [169] He suggested four proposals for reconciliation between Korea and Japan:

> a) The people of Korea and Japan solemnly stand before God and pray to find His providence and make it achieved as He provided.
> b) Let 's have an exchange program of the church and other organization leaders to improve correct comprehension of the present problems.
> c) Let 's review the past history and develop a firm resolution not to repeat what was done in the past.
> d) Let 's encourage and advise each government to solve this problem with their best sincerity and honesty.[170]

This was the first international peace seminar led by Korean Christians in Korean history and the first inter-church reconciliation seminar between Korea and Japan.

The Second International Peace Conference in Tokyo, Japan (1966)

The second peace conference for reconciliation between the Korean and Japanese churches was held on May 13-15, 1966, in Tokyo.[171] The original name of this seminar was "The Fifth Mennonite Central Committee Peace Section" which was sponsored by the Annual Christian Youth Peace Seminar. Fifty-

---

[169] *Brochure of the Program for Reconciliation Seminar*, Korea MCC, October 28-29, 1965, found in the file entitled "Japan-Korea Relations," Box 1, File 41, in the "MCC Korean Files, AMC."

[170] Carl Beck, "Korean Talk Reconciliation Hope for Meeting with Japan," *The Mennonite*, March 15, 1966.

[171] See the paper of "Reconciliation in International Aspects" presented by Chang-Woo Rhee, found in the file entitled "Japan-Korea Relations," Box 1, File 41, in the "MCC Korean Files, AMC."

one persons participated in this seminar including eight representatives from Korea.[172] The main subject of the seminar was reconciliation between Japan and Korea, and the main speakers were Dagashi Saburo, professor of Tokyo University and professor Ki-Dong Chang, dean of the graduate school of Taegu university. [173] Professor Saburo's lecture title was "Condition of Reconciliation" and professor Chang's lecture title was "For the Reconciliation between Japan and Korea."[174]

An article in *The Canadian Mennonite* commented on 'the Japanese-Korean encounter" as follows:

> There was much frank talk and a clear discussion of issues. There was some bewilderment but more understanding on the part of the Japanese participants concerning the continuing antagonism and fear of Korean Christians toward their Japanese counter parts. There were confessions, tears, and the joining of hearts in prayers…As a result of this meeting the Japanese committee has decided to invite a sizable contingent of Koreans on the leadership level and widely representative both geographically and denominationally to meet with a similar Japanese group in early spring, 1967.[175]

Korea's MCC workers also led prayer meetings with Christian

---

[172] Carl Beck, "Korean Church Leaders Ponder Peace," *The Canadian Mennonite*, February 22, 1966, p.8.

[173] By the report of *the 7th Arrangement Committee of Peace Seminar*, January 27, 19966, found in the file entitled "Japan-Korea Relations," Box 1, File 41, in the "MCC Korean Files, AMC," eight Korean representatives were KieDong Chang, SooShik Im, GilSang Lim, ChulDong Hahn, WonHak Son, LeeBong Kim, SangWhal Lee, and BoYoon Beck.

[174] Carl Beck, "Japan-Korea Encounter Bring Pleas for Reconciliation," *The Canadian Mennonite*, Tuesday, July 19, 1966, p.1.

[175] *Brief Minutes of the Report on Seminar: 5th Christian Youth Seminar in Japan*, Korea MCC, July 16,1966, found in the file entitled "Japan-Korea Relations," Box 1, File 41, in the "MCC Korean Files, AMC."

leaders for the seminar, on the last Thursday of every month. These meetings planted peace education and reconciliation in Korean Christian leaders. Participants included pastors, professors, and social movement leaders. Through these prayer meetings, Korea MCC planned lectures and discussions on peace and reconciliation. Korea MCC had twelve prayer meetings between December 1965 and November 1966. The themes of the prayer meetings were as follows:[176]

Although Beck and Goossen planned to send 10 Korean representatives to a third peace seminar in 1967, their plans were not realized because of economic and other problems. [177] However, MCC's efforts in the peace movement had a great influence on building reconciliation between Japan and Korea. The expenses of both international peace conferences and youth work camps were covered mostly by MCC. [178] Some colleges located in the Kyungbook area also planned youth peace reconciliation seminars with the help of MCC.[179]

Significance of MCC's Reconciliation Policy

The 1960s in Korea were an era of anti-Japanese movement because of the normalization treaty between Korea and Japan. In addition, the government strengthened the anti-communism campaign against North Korea and the Pro-Pyongyang

---

[176] Ibid., p.6.

[177] I have adopted this table from the reports of *Brief Minutes of the Prayer Meeting* (between 1st and 12th meeting), found in the file entitled "Japan-Korea Relations," Box 1, File41, in the "MCC Korean Files, AMC."

[178] By *Dong Keun Lee's Letter to Japan MCC*, March 6, 1967, speakers from Korea were MyungShik Ro-Reconciliation in Historical Viewpoint, Pyung-Goo Ro- "Reconciliation in Theological Viewpoint, KwangHoon Kim-" Cooperating to Build the Kingdom of God," Taiwanese pastor, Ting Shin's Sermons.

[179] *Henry W. Goossen's Letter of Invitation and Guarantee*, May 8, 1967, found in the file entitled "Japan-Korea Relations," Box 1, File 41, in the "MCC Korea File, AMC."

Federation of Korean Residents in Japan. For this reason, Koreans or foreigners could not even think of a peace and reconciliation movement.

There are three reasons MCC as a foreign organization succeeded with its reconciliation policies in Korea. First, MCC has built a positive image since arriving in Korea. Both Korean Christians and the Korean government had a favorable impression of MCC. This was because of their work in social services, economic development programs, and orphans and children's education. Secondly, Mennonites brought advanced mediation skills which were evident in the two programs. Because the Japanese and Koreans worked together in service, the work camps created an atmosphere for the most effective kind of dialogue to take place. They also held the first international peace conference at which each side understood the other and resolve conflict. Lastly, MCC's headquarters in both countries supported inter-church fellowship and dialogue between Japanese and Korean Christians.

There are several ways that MCC's reconciliation policies were significant in Korean Christian history. The reconciliation work camps were the first interchurch youth fellowships and dialogues. Secondly, the international peace conferences also were the first inter-denominational peace seminars for reconciliation between Japanese and Korean Christians. Finally, both reconciliation work camps and international peace conferences became pillars of the Asian youth reconciliation work camp.

Conclusion

Thirty years have passed since MCC implemented their reconciliation policies between Korea and Japan, and 25 years since they withdrew. Yet for 25 years, although some historical conflicts between Korea and Japan were eliminated, both countries continue to deal with previous, and recently formed conflicts.

<Table 11>   Themes of Prayer Meetings

Meeting	Date	Topic	Participants	Place
1st	Dec.30,'65	Prayer for reconciliation between Korea and Japan and the peaceful reunification between South and North Korea	8	YMCA (Taegu)
2nd	Jan. 27, '66	Bible reading (Heb. 11:19) and prayer for the modernization of Korea, reconciliation between the political parties reconciliation between Japan and Korea, the peace of Vietnam and India-Pakistan, and the reconciliation between Liberal China and Red China	16	YMCA (Taegu)
3rd	Feb.24, '66	Bible reading (Matt. 5:13-16,21-24) and prayer for Christians' good influence to the world	9	YMCA (Taegu)
4th	March 31, '66	Bible reading (John 14:27) and prayer for the prayer meeting, Korean churches, and international peace (Vietnam situation and reconciliation between Japan and Korea)	9	YMCA (Taegu)
5th	April 28, '66	Prof. Chang Woo Rhee's lecture on "South Vietnam Situation" and prayer for peace	8	YMCA (Taegu)
6th	May 26, '66	Bible reading (Acts 1:1-11) and discussion on "Farm Problem"	17	MCC Office (Taegu)
7th	June 30, '66	Bible reading (I Cor. 13:13) and Dr. Llyod Ramseyer's lecture on "Christian Love as a Guiding Principle"	26	YMCA (Taegu)
8th	July 28, '66	Bible reading (Col. 1:19-23; Matt. 26:52; Gal 5:15) and Rev. Soon Woo Hong's two lectures: (1) Relationship between Japan and Korea based on the Bible (2) Historical Relationship between Japan and Korea	10	YMCA (Taegu)
9th	Aug. 25, '66	Bible reading (Rom. 12:3-8) and Prof. Sung Hyuck Kim's lecture on "Reconciliation between New and Old Testament Theologies"	13	YMCA (Taegu)
10th		no source		
11th	Oct. 27, '66	Bible reading (II Cor. 5:16-21) and Rev. Goossen's lecture on "The Ministry of Reconciliation	17	MCC Office (Taegu)
12th	Nov. 24, '66	Bible reading (Gal. 5:24-26) and Lyle Troyer's lecture on "Pax Service"	15	YMCA (Taegu)

First, the problems related to the Japanese-born Korean people's citizenship right are not finished. Although the Japanese government abolished the fingerprinting record of Korean-Japanese people, they do not yet have the right to vote in local elections. Furthermore, it is difficult for them to get a job in Japanese society, even though they graduated from a professional education program.

Secondly, the Japanese government's distorted view of its colonial history has left an obstacle of governmental reconciliation between Korea and Japan. Many public officials supported Japanese colonial rule in Asia until now. On November 14, 1995, Etoy Takami, the Japanese Minister of Government Administration, was replaced by Murayama Tomiichi, the Japanese Premier. This was because he spoke out in support of the Japanese colonial rule. In 1995, Murayama officially wrote to Kim Young-Sam, South Korean President an apology for the annexation in 1910 and the colonial rule.[180] Currently, the conflict between Japan and South Korea continuously escalates because of the Dokdo/Takeshima disputes. Dokdo is Korean territory. However, since the colonial period Japan has insisted that this is their territory. Korean government rejected Japanese research vessels to Dokdo Island due to historical distortions by the Japanese government.

Thirdly, the comfort women issue between Japan and Korea is also a serious social and political conflict. Comfort women are young females of various ethnic and national backgrounds and social circumstances. They were forced into sexual slavery by the Japanese Imperial Army before and during the Second World War. The issue of Comfort Women in the context of violence against women and patriarchal sexual culture and militarism became of international interest. This attracted the attention of the U.S. Congress and the United Nations. In September 2006, the U.S. Congress passed a resolution on women subjected to sexual slavery during World War Two on Wednesday. The resolution reminded the international community of Japan's wartime atrocities. The Korean Council for Women Drafted for Military Sexual Slavery by Japan and other NGOs have appealed for compensation for victims to the Japanese government. Their main demands are as follows:

    1. the Japanese government admits the forced draft of

---

[180] *Chun Ihl Kim's Letter to Carl Beck,* January 13, 1966, found in the "Japan-Korea Relations," Box 1, File 41, in the "MCC Korea File, AMC."

Korean women as comfort women;
2. a public apology be made for this;
3. all barbarities be fully disclosed;
4. a memorial be raised for the victims;
5. the survivors or their bereaved families be compensated;
6. the historical education system must integrate these facts constantly so that such misdeeds do not be repeated in the future.

Fourth, the anti-war and anti-nuclear weapons movement between Korea and Japan based on disarmament is the most significant future task for the peaceful reunification of the Korean peninsula and North East Asia security. In addition, a study of the effective disarmament of the US Army in Korea and Japan will also be a very significant future task. Fifth, in order to protect the Pacific's environment from various types of pollution including Russia's nuclear wastes, both countries must work together for green peace. In the future, a youth work camp for the environment-protection movement would also be a good policy for reconciliation.

Lastly, conference groups like MCC are important to establish reconciliation and peace movements in both countries. MCC's mediation skills and the Japanese Mennonite churches' efforts, like the previous reconciliation efforts planted in Korea and Japan, will play a significant role in new peace settlements between these two countries, and in Asia, as well.

4

RELIGIOUS PEACEBUILDING TOWARD SOUTH KOREA

82

Introduction

As I wrote in the previous chapter, Korea has a long-term conflict which was formed under the pre- and post-Cold War system, for example, the conflict between Japan and Korea caused by Japanese colonial rule, the conflict between North and South Korea caused by the Korean War, the conflict between U.S. soldiers stationed in Korea and Korean victims by the U.S. soldiers 'criminal action, and so forth.

Therefore, I would like to suggest the most important and possible policies to the peacebuilding process in a Korean contemporary context. To begin, Korea needs a religious approach to the transformation of historical conflicts - the Korean Reunification Movement, a reconciliation between Korea and Japan, the Anti-War and Anti-Nuclear Weapons Movement, and the Criminal Justice Movement to eliminate antagonism between the U.S. Army stationed in Korea and the Korean victims. Other significant religious approaches are the Teen-to-Teen Mediation Program and the Green Peace Movement. All the programs I have suggested are possible through Korean Christians and the Mennonite Church.

The Necessity of the Mennonite Network for Korea's Peace (MNKP) and Inter-Relationship

There are several reasons for establishing MNKP in Washington D.C. and Seoul (or in the Abba Shalom community located in Gangwon province -a Korean Mennonite Christian community)[181]. A geographical peace network in Asia can be promoted by this peace mission agency. Since Korea is surrounded by powerful Asian nations such as China, Russia, and Japan, Korea needs to recognize these countries and have some sort of international interest in these countries. MNKP assistance and compromises need to be made to resolve the Korean conflict between North and South Korea, as well as the conflict between South Korea and Japan. Therefore, with the help of MCC's missionaries, currently in Japan, China, and Russia, a way to promote the MNKP Project as a way to use religious peace building is possible.

Second, Korea has historically experienced many types of conflicts and wars involving Ancient China, Japanese Imperialism and the Korean War. As a result of this, Korean Christians have recognized these problems and are teaching others how to resolve such conflicts through peace. This is why MNKP is an organization that plays a very significant part in religious approaches to peacebuilding. Lastly, politically and economically, South Korea has a democratic government and is progressing economically. In addition, many Korean churches have developed. The South Korean government and Korean churches can form a strong foundation for resolving the Asian conflict. Therefore, I am sure and confident that the MCC is the most influential peace mission agent in giving knowledge of peace to the Korean churches and the Korean government.

MNKP has two kinds of peace missions, including the Washington Korea Peace Network (WKNP). The other is called the International Korea Peace Network (IKPN). WKPN should be set up in Washington, D.C. because it is the capital of the United States. This allows WKNP to obtain information and resources to begin peace building. Additionally, there are many peace-related conflict resolution organizations in Washington D.C. that can work with WKPN. Finally, there are many Korean American churches near Washington, D.C. who can sponsor this

---

[181] There are some Mennonite oriented leaders in the Abba Shalom Community (e.g., Rev. Eee-Bong Kim, Rev. Yoon-Shik Lee, Rev. Hong-Kyung Jin, etc.).

project.

<Figure 4>   Washington Korea Peace Network (WKPN)

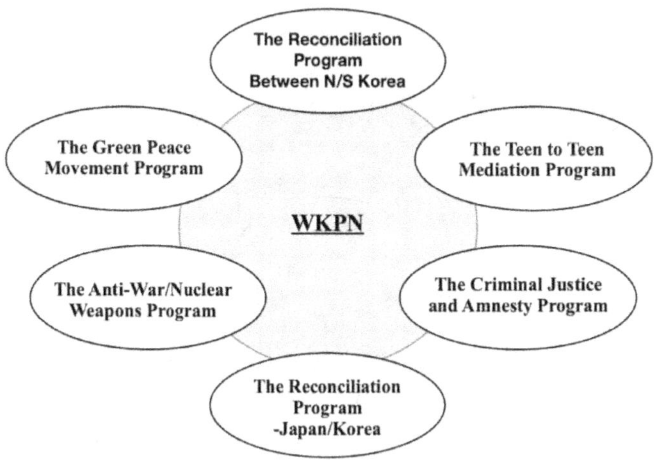

WKPN has some sub-organizations for the peace building project as illustrated in <Figure 4>: the reconciliation program between North and South Korea, the reconciliation program between Korea and Japan, the Teen Mediation Program, the criminal justice/Amnesty Program, the Anti-War and Nuclear Weapons Movement, the broadcasting mission program, and the Green Peace Movement Program. Each program can be supported by a committee, consisting of the Korean-American churches, the American churches and MCC.

IKPN is the international network of WKPN and is located in Seoul or Gangwon province, Korea. The inter-relationship is the same as <Figure 5> which is linked with the Korean MCC and other countries as well. IKPN Projects can be used in Seoul, the capital of South Korea. It has many multi-channel channels for information about Asian peace conflict resolution programs as well as many churches and organizations that sponsor them. It will be very helpful to have a combined system between WKPN and IKPN. IKPN has seven other programs, including MNKP. Each program will be supported by a committee, which consists of Korean churches, American churches, and MCC members.

<Figure 5>   **International Korea Peace Network (IKPN)**

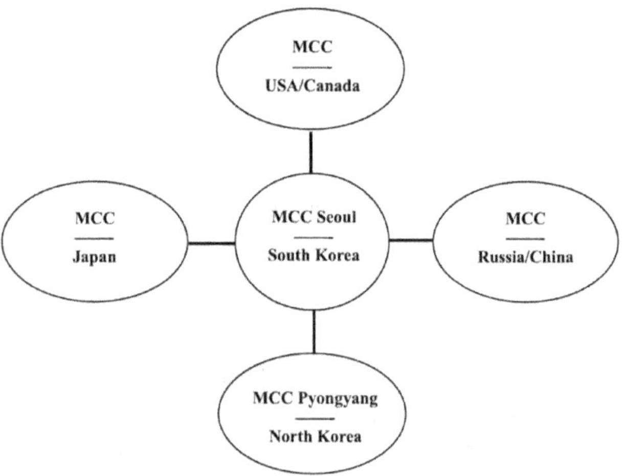

Realizable Peace Mission Programs and Sub-Organizations

1. The Reconciliation Program between North and South Korea

I think the following proposals are necessary projects for Korean society. As a result of the passion and missionary programs Mennonite missionaries demonstrated in Korea, I think these will be good projects that can easily be practiced in Korea again.

<Project 1>
Title: Material Aid Program for Starving North Korean Children

Background: The terrible natural disaster last summer (1995) displaced half a million people and left 100,000 families homeless. Out of the 500,000 displaced people, 55,000 are children under five. According to a recent on-the-spot review by the Food and Agriculture Organization of the United Nations (FAO) and World Food Program (WFP), it is estimated that, until the next harvest in October 1996, 33,750 tons of cereals (maize, cornmeal, wheat, and rice) are required in emergency food aid for 500,000 flood victims.

Since 2001, North Korean agricultural production has improved. Through favorable weather conditions and increased fertilizer application (from international aid), improvement of irrigation facilities, and electricity from the city, North Korea's cereal production, including potatoes in cereal equivalent, is forecast at 4.16 million tonnes.

According to the FAO/WFP report on October 30, 2003, "the cereal deficit in 2003/04 (November/October) is estimated at 944,000 tons. With commercial imports estimated at 100,000 tons, confessional imports at 300,000 tones mainly from the Republic of Korea, and anticipated food aid at 140,000 tones, there remains a deficit of 404,000 tones which needs to be covered by additional food aid and confessional imports."
Terms: Long-term project (5-10 years)
Workers: Co-work with Mennonite U.N. workers
Organization: Needs a special committee consisting of Mennonite churches

Cooperation: FAO, WFP, Korean Red Cross…FAO and WFP have special offices in Pyongyang. They distribute material aid sent directly from many countries to starving North Koreans.

When North Korea had a terrible natural disaster in 1995, I organized a fundraising concert for starving North Korean children. The concert was sponsored by Eastern Mennonite University and James Madison University at EMU Seminary Chapel. We made $2,000, which we sent to the United Nations World Food Program. Dr. John Paul Leaderach assisted us directly send these monies. I strongly recommend that MCC help starving North Korean children. Since 1996, MCC has distributed material aid to North Korean adults and children, including food, clothing, and newborn kits. MCC has also helped with agricultural development in North Korea; they have sent several workers to Pyongyang. MCC farms were visited by North Korean representatives, such as Mr. Hyung-Chul Lee; he is the Ambassador of North Korea to the U.N. MCC also sent English teachers to North Korea, but recently, their activity ceased due to the North Korean government 's rejection of their visa status. The rejection of their visa status is largely due to political tensions between the North Korean government and the American government.

<10 Rules for North Korean Mission>

Listed below are 10 rules for the MCC's North Korean mission:
1) First, search for a specific program that promotes economic and social development, which cannot be used for military aid.
2) Mid-range program of 3–5 years is much better than a long-term program because the political situation is unstable. If there is a long-term program, this work can be stopped before completion.
3) Do not become involved with political groups or partisan activities while in North Korea. Position yourself as a humanitarian assistance program. If you are involved in too many political actions, work can be canceled in the future, due to political shifts.
4) Do not use many channels when networking with North

Koreans; use fewer channels when networking. This would become complicated with North Korea, due to the hierarchical/ military regime of North Korea.

5) Do not become involved in American government interests toward North Korean policy; stay focused on the sense of a North Korean mission. For example, George W. Bush declared North Korea part of the Axis of Evil. Focus on MCC's original mission statement instead of the political interests of the American government.

6) Through social and economic development programs gain credibility from the North Korean government.

7) If you can start a successful program, with the credibility of the North Korean government, MCC can have a peace and justice and aid program, which MCC wants to have in the future.

8) Develop visiting and exchanging programs. For example, by inviting North Korean leaders and students to visit North Korea with American leaders, for instance, we can share techniques (especially agricultural techniques), conflict resolution skills, a youth reconciliation work camp, co-hosting an international peace seminar, etc.

9) Develop international conflict resolution and peace seminars. There should be a neutral place for this seminar, such as Russia, China, Korea, and Japan, as these countries have connections with North Korean leaders. We can invite these leaders directly and indirectly to these neutral places to attend seminars.

10) Help starving North Koreans directly in North Korea, through the long-term program. Try to transform North Korean society through humanitarian and peace-oriented MCC programs.

<Project 2>
Title: Christian Child Care Program

Background: One of the most serious problems is food shortages for children. According to the conclusions of the nutritional assessment published in March/April of this year by the WFP, "young children attending nurseries and kindergartens have been protected from food shortages. However, without adequate food assistance, the population's nutritional situation can only decline." In addition, Vitamins D, B, and C are thought to be inadequate. WFP also emphasized that "some 11,800 tonnes of fortified cereal mix is needed for distribution, through kindergartens and nurseries, of 150 grams/day per capita to 25 percent of the 2.1 million children under five who are in the most vulnerable stages of malnutrition." The establishment of nursery schools and the sending of material aid is also part of the urgent mission program.

Terms: Long-term project

Workers: Needs one or two Mennonite U.N. workers. Becoming a U.N. worker to enter North Korea.

Organization: A special committee consisting of the Mennonite Churches and Korean churches is needed.

Cooperation: FAO, WFP, and Red Cross workers stationed in Pyongyang.

MCC has a worldwide program to assist starving children. There are many workers who want to help children. This cultural exchange program is effective, and it is possible. MCC will be able to invite North Korean children to visit the United States. Recently, MCC involved itself with an invitation program for Iraqi students to come here to the United States.

<Project 3>

Title: Exchanging Fellow and Research Program in Conflict Analysis and Resolution – between Kim Il-Sung University and Mennonite Schools (EMS, Goshen College, AMBS, and so on)

Background: Kim Il-Sung University is a unique and intellectual center for training future leaders for the development of North Korea. The idea and nature of Kim Il-Sung University are based on "Ju-che Ideology" which was systematized by former president Kim Il-Sung 's philosophy of social communism. Otherwise, universities and colleges in Korea are based on democracy. Unfortunately, since the Korean

War, neither country has conducted any kind of fellowship exchanges or research program exchanges. The exchange of fellows and the research of conflict analysis and resolution by MCC will be a new era of the Messianic peace mission in the Korean peninsula. The program can be a joint project with Quaker school peace-oriented schools. MCC's conflict resolution program also will be helpful for human rights issues in North Korea.

According to *Country Reports on Human Rights Practices-2005* completed by the U.S. Department of State, the following is released by the Bureau of Democracy, Human Rights, and Labor

March 8, 2006. The following human rights abuses have been documented or alleged over the years: abridgment of the right to change the government extrajudicial killings, disappearances, and arbitrary detention, including many political prisoners harsh and life-threatening prison conditions torture forced abortions and infanticide in prisons lack of an independent judiciary and fair trials denial of freedom of speech, press, assembly, and association government attempts to control all information denial of freedom of religion, freedom of movement, and worker rights severe punishment of some repatriated refugees

Terms: Long-term

Workers: Co-Work with U.N. workers in Pyongyang and future Mennonite U.N. workers.

Organization: Need a special committee consisting of the Mennonite Peace Committee and specialists in conflict analysis and resolution.

Cooperation: FAO, WFP, and peace-oriented institutes

2. The Reconciliation Program
between Korea and Japan

Title: The Second Reconciliation Work Camp & International Peace Conference

Background: MCC fostered reconciliation between the South Koreans and the Japanese through the international reconciliation work camp (1964-1968) and international peace conference (1964-1968). However, it is time to plan the second MCC reconciliation project. This is because both countries have multi-faceted conflicts and these conflicts require more kinds of reconciliation and mediation skills that the MCC has accumulated from other countries. The recent hot conflicts are as follows: the distortion of Japan's colonial rule, the possession of Dok-Do Island, the enfranchisement of the Korean-Japanese, the indemnity of comfort women during colonial rule, and so on, but relations between Korea and Japan are not always so dark. Both countries hope to reconcile with one another through big events, such as 2002 World Cup Joint Open, sponsored by the Federation International de Football Association (FIFA). Therefore, the efforts and comments by both countries' MCC workers, including previous missionaries, are very significant for this second reconciliation project.

Terms: Long-term

Workers: One or two Mennonite workers in Korea

Organization: Need a special committee consisting of Mennonite churches, Japan MCC, Korean MCC, and other Christian groups.

Cooperation: Joint with Japan MCC as well as local Mennonite churches.

Recently, MCC coordinated an inter-visit program between Korean Mennonites and Japanese Mennonites. There have been antagonistic tensions between the two countries since the territorial dispute over Dok-Do Island began. MCC can be a mediator, and has a program to eliminate this antagonistic relationship.

3. Teen to Teen Mediation Program

Title: Teen to Teen Mediation Program

Background: Asian schools' counseling systems for teens with problems are very hierarchical. Sometimes the problem-solving process can be affected by the typical Korean "top to bottom" communication hierarchy system - the principal, the council of teachers, the student's administrator, the counselor, and then the student. In a mediation structure, many students can be troubled by hierarchical interruptions by the principal, counselor, and colleague. We intend to gain some effect by training and practicing "teen-to-teen mediation by teen mediators." It is not difficult to give senior students opportunities to help troubled teens younger than them through this project. This is an excellent idea because seniors may have experienced the same problems when they were younger. Teens are most likely to listen to people of their own age rather than adults who may not understand. This is because of the generation gap between adults and teens. Not only is there a generation gap between the two, but the society teens now live in has changed, and will continue to evolve over the years. Although adults may be wise or think they have all the answers, teens face different problems and environments.

Generally, the age of a Korean middle school student is 13 to 15. High school students are between 16 and 18. Korea's middle school grades are from 7th through 9th grade, and high school is from 10th through 12th grade. Korea needs many teen mediators because of Korea's education system. Korea has many types of schools. These include schools for art, engineering, government, education, and even ambassadors. According to the education statistics for 1995 published by the Department of Education in South Korea, there are 2,481,848 students and 99,931 teachers.

This program can be a nationwide joint project with the Department of Education. This program can also be an international joint mediation program with teens from around the world. Depending on the range of the program, MCC and the Korean government can have national or international sub-organizations, for example, the International Teen Mediation

Program under WKPN in Washington, D.C., and IKNP in Seoul, Korea, Korean Teen Mediation Training Center, which can be sponsored by the Department of Education, Middle, and High School Teen Mediation Training Association that can be sponsored by the Department of Education: Council of Teen Mediation, Christian School Association for the Teen Mediation Program, Teen Mediation Group and Circle Association.

There are many benefits for teens participating in the program. Some of these benefits are that teens can go to teen mediation group meetings to get help, seniors who were involved in this program may get involved again in some sort of mediation group in college but at a higher level, seniors who did the mediation program in high school may be interested in majoring in things that relate to mediation. For example, they may discover they would like to study to become an ambassador or mediator. From this group, teens will gain a better understanding of each other, and so will parents who have troubled teens of their own.

Terms: Long term

Workers: Two or three MCC peacemakers

Organization: Needs special committee consisting of an MCC specialist in mediation, Korean church leaders, governmental staff, schools and school directors.

Cooperation: MCC, and the Department of Education, middle schools, and high schools.

Mediation program has been introduced by Quakers and Mennonites in Korea, especially KAC, they are a good way to introduce mediation skills based on Mennonites in North Korea. We must also consider the internal values like an employer and employee, store owner and customer, and victims and offenders of mediation in Korea. Traditionally in Korea, mediation skills are in the form of the elderly or those formally trained; many Korean people need mediation skills from their peer groups. Some Korean teenagers are experiencing isolation from certain individuals in their classrooms and school clubs, which is called "Wang-Da (bullying)." This has led to an increase in teen suicides, so we need teenagers with mediation skills to be involved in these peer groups.

4. Green Peace Movement Program

Title: Asian Mennonite Youth Green Peace Work Camp

Background: Although Northeast Asian counties achieved economic development quickly and gained political predominance on the international scene, environmental pollution has grown, creating serious problems for government and industry. On September 30, 1996, the South Korean government discussed establishing an environmental cooperation organization with other Northeast Asian countries. This included North Korea, China, Japan, Russia, Mongolia, and others. The environmental component of Asian Youth education is a very important factor. The MCC, through its organizational experience and ecotheology, might initiate an exchange of Asian youth with the U.S.-based Amish Community. Green Peace Youth Camp will be one of the most realizable projects in the world. The fragile environment and current ecological crisis on the Korean peninsula need attention. This camp can happen annually or bi-annually and alternate between Korea and other Northeast Asian countries.

Terms: Long-term

Workers: Co-work with the Asian MCC workers.

Organization: A special committee made up of members of both the Asian Mennonite Church and the Korean MCC is needed.

Cooperation: Mennonite Conference Youth Ministries, Asian MCC Church, and other Asian Green Peace action groups.

This program is supposed to be more developed in Korea, recently Frontier Mission, which is related with KAC in Korea, has planned reconciliation or peace work camp in third world countries. Frontier Mission has served East Timor and Afghanistan for helping with community development and starving people. Similarly to material aid, I think the green peace movement in Asia is a very good program.

5. Restorative Justice and Mediation Program

Title: Conflict Transformation Between U.S. Military Personnel Stationed in Korea and Korean Civilians.

Background: This program is one of the most positive programs for initiating restorative justice and reconciliation from an international perspective. This program is to resolve both explicit conflict and underlying animosity between victim and offender according to the Status of the United States Armed Forces (SOFA) in Korea. This conflict appears most often in the form of Korean victim vs. U.S. soldier, but it can also be U.S. soldier vs. Korean offender. The SOFA covers facilities and areas, criminal jurisdiction, labor, civil justice, finance, commerce, transportation and the entry and exit of U.S. forces in Korea. However, the Korean SOFA is unclear about the punishment for U.S. soldiers who violate the SOFA laws. It is also unclear about the legal restitution to Korean civilians when this occurs. Because this has become such an important issue in Korea, there is a significant need for skillful and experienced third-party mediators and peacemakers, which the Mennonites can provide. Only with these individuals trained and ready to take on the rough task of bringing both victim and offender to the table of peace will the situation improve.

Terms: Long-term

Workers: Term of two or three Mennonite peacemakers or mediators.

Organization: A special committee made up of members of the Mennonite Church, the Korean MCC and the restorative justice group is needed.

Cooperation: Joint operation between MCC mediation and reconciliation practitioners, the Korean justice community and Japan MCC.

Korean President Moo-Hyun Roh met with President George

Bush on September 13th in Washington, D.C. at The White House. The Korean military's wartime control was discussed. By 2012, both countries had agreed to yield command of troops from the U.S. to Korea. Recently, the South Korean government expected this to occur earlier, in 2009. However, conservative groups in Korea object to the Korean government's policy of taking wartime command of the military from the U.S. At this time, the Pentagon is mainly focused on the crisis in the Middle East and Korean Peninsula, thus keeping many forces stationed in Asia. Many scholars have understood Korean government policy; but they suggest several preconditions such as: one is to keep a national security agreement relationship between Korea and the U.S. The other is high-tech military equipment needs to be supplied to the Korean Peninsula, under the dismissal of the U.S. military.

I think it is very interesting that the Korean government along with many scholars prefer to have a security relationship between the two countries under the dismissal of the U.S. military. While the American government will accept this dismissal, it will demand high-tech military equipment to be used by South Korea. U. S. officials would then ask the Korean government to purchase American-produced military equipment.

6. Mennonite Anti-War and Anti-Nuclear Weapons Project

Title: Northeast Asian Mennonite Disarmament Action Conference

Background: Since the end of the Korean Civil War, tension between North and South Korea have not de-escalated. This continued tension has created an arms race on the Korean peninsula and has the potential to create another major war with nuclear consequences. North Korea has tried to produce nuclear weapons despite strong sanctions by the International Atomic

Energy Agency (IAEA). Meanwhile, South Korea possesses high-tech arms bought from both the U.S. and Russian governments. In addition, the Japanese government increased its defense budget to $492 billion in 1997. This was with the rationalization that they needed enhanced "security" in the event of a North Korean offensive. The four major powers - the U.S., Japan, China, and Russia – have all increased their defense budgets in the name of the Asian Pacific New Security Order. This very volatile environment is a tragedy waiting to happen.

Therefore, we need a disarmament conference along with an understanding of conflict resolution, non-violence, and peace theology. Only in this context can hostilities and antagonisms between Koreas be reduced. Transforming the Demilitarized Zone on the 38th Parallel into an International Peace Park (or Peace Zone) will bring much needed change. The Japan MCC and the American MCC are key players in this initiative.

Terms: Long-term

Workers: Team of Mennonites from all the major powers in the Asian Pacific region as well as other Christian Peace Action Groups

Organization: A special committee made up of members of both the Mennonite church and the Korean MCC

Cooperation: For us to organize the disarmament information network with MCC, Japan MCC, Quaker groups, and American disarmament groups

Since 2006 North Korea test-fired a medium-range ballistic missile into Japanese airspace, yet this action was not geared towards South Korea, but the U.S. The Bush administration "has sought to pressure North Koreans back to negotiations, cracking down on Pyongyang's suspected counterfeiting and money-laundering operations by persuading international financial institutions to do business with the country." (See Washington Post August 29th, 2006 page A10)

I think that if the U.S. uses political pressure on the North Koreans (along with economic sanctions) to achieve certain goals, this may only lead to the closing of communication channels. All of these actions may lead North Koreans to develop nuclear weapons for self-defense. We are supposed to continue six party talks, not by U.S. leadership. Many professional scholars of East Asia worry about the U.S. becoming an empire towards the Middle East and North Korea. Therefore, MCC can offer a mediation program focused on current issues on the Korean Peninsula.

Also, the MCC can have a special seminar focused on Conscientious Objections (COs). Recently, many young Korean men have become conscientious objectors, although the Korean government does not accept their action or situation. According to the increase in Korean COs, the Korean department of Justice has become interested. Radical groups and lawyers support them. Someday the Korean government will accept alternative service substitutes for the COs. It will take a long time, but most young Korean COs are in prison. COs are one of the main areas of MCC's faith. As a result, MCC will be able to offer internal and international seminars and workshops on COs in Korea and Asia.

7. International Urban Ministry Program

Title: Inner-City Ministry and Homeless Experience for Youths

Background: APPA Center was founded in 1996 to serve the poor and low-income persons and to foster conflict resolution and racial harmony in the Washington metropolitan area including Washington, D.C., downtown Baltimore, MD and downtown Richmond, VA. APPA also founded the Fourth Street Community Fellowship (FSCF) in Washington, D.C. which is a congregation consisting of homeless people. The FSCF goals are to end homelessness, conflict resolution, racial harmony, and our multicultural and multiracial society. Our main program is helping the poor with material support, reconciling and integrating diverse groups, and community development. We advocate for social justice and peace. FSCF is affiliated with the Virginia Mennonite Conference. APPA also established the

Center for Racial Conflict Resolution in 1988. The focus of this center is the growth of mediation and arbitration within the community.

Recently, APPA and FSCF has joined the nation-wide summer and winter mission program. During the summer, 400 young people visited the APPA center for a 1-week inner-city mission program from all over the nation. During the winter months, college students come to the APPA center for a 2-week program. Through these inner-city mission programs, students feed homeless people and participate in community development, racial harmony efforts, and leadership training. Each week, 15-30 young people will be in an inner-city mission program. MCC can therefore join this program with APPA and FSCF to train Asian Mennonites in our nation's capital.

Terms: Short-term.

Workers: Team of Mennonites from all the major powers in the Asian Pacific region as well as other Christian Inner-City Ministry Groups.

Organization: A special committee made up of Mennonite Church, Korean and Asian MCC members.

Cooperation: For us to organize the Inner-City Ministry Network with MCC, Asian MCC, and local Anabaptist groups (which are groups involved in inner-city mission groups).

Conclusion

In the pre- and post-cold wars, Asian conflicts were influenced by imperialistic aggressions and economic dependence more than internal forces. There are two important Asian conflict structures: the political conflict structures—imperialistic aggressions by Japan and Western big powers, inner civil wars, and inner revolutions according to the dictatorships of bureaucratic and military governments and the socio-economic conflict structures—economic injustice, racial conflict, class conflict, and religious conflict. Although these types of conflict are very similar to African conflicts, the methodologies and processes behind conflict resolution are different. While modern Africa is in the period of conflict escalation, Asia is in the transition phase of conflict and resolution. Since former Russian President Gorbachov's proclamation of 'perestroika' (reformation) and 'glasnost'(openness) Asian communism has collapsed, and with the Association of Southeast Asian Nations (ASEAN)' appearance, Asian countries' economic growth is progressing significantly. This has provided Asia with the opportunity to overcome its social, political, and economic conflicts. In addition, Asian traditional cultures and religious-philosophical peace thoughts including Confucianism, Buddhism, and Taoism are also potential sources for the study of mediation skills.182 Christian thoughts of peace and love have played a significant role in Asian society.

I am sure MCC is the best peace-loving mission agency. MCC's support for South Korea's peacebuilding will encourage Korean Christianity, which is anxious to realize the 'Messianic peace mission' to be a new mission issue of the twenty-first century. However, Korean Christianity needs to understand the importance of MCC and Asian Mennonite churches and cooperate to establish religious peacemaking, and peacebuilding.

---

182 Adam Curle is one of the most prominent scholars studying mediation skills based on Buddhism. This is like John Paul Lederarch's study of African cultures. See Adam Curle's book, *Tools For Transformation: A Personal Study* (1990:Hawthorn Press) and John Paul Lederarch's book, *Preparing For Peace: Conflict Transformation Across Cultures* (1995:Syrscuse University Press).

5

JUBILEE THEOLOGY AS A RESTORATION OF HEMANITY BETWEEN NORTH AND SOUTH KOREA

Introduction

The first Jubilee of Korea was the liberation from Japanese colonial rule on August 15, 1945, like Israel's exodus from Egypt. Japan's cruel 36 years rule was one of the most significant causes of antagonism between Japan and Korea. On August 15th, 1995, Korea observed the second Jubilee, and the third jubilee will be in the year 2045. Tragically, without the joy of the first Korean Jubilee, the Korean people were faced with antagonism between North and South Korea from the Korean War that started in June 1950. Many Korean churches and denominations expected that the second Jubilee year would become the foundation stone of peaceful Korean reunification. Some denominations declared that the second Jubilee year should be "the year of reunification." However, this dream was not realized. Therefore, they hope that the Korean War Jubilee could mark reconciliation between North and South. This was on June 25, 2000 (the datum point according to the beginning of the war) or August 8th, 2003 (the end of the war).

The most difficult and disturbing issue confounding Korean peaceful reunification is the antagonism between North Korea' communism and South Korea's anti-communist capitalism. For this reason, Korean Christianity should know what the most effective method is to eliminate our hostility toward the peaceful reunification of Korea is through Christ's forgiveness and love of the enemy. Therefore, I want to study the theory of conflict resolution based on the Jubilee of reunification as well as the basis of historical antagonism resulting from Japanese imperialism and the Korean War. We need to consider Yahweh's 'shalom', Christ's 'eirene', and Christ's conflict-solving skills as they relate to personal, interpersonal, interpersonal, and group antagonisms.

The Possibility of Korea's Jubilee Theology

Yahweh's Declaration of Jubilee as a Peace Theology

It is very important that Korea's Jubilee is interpreted in the context of Old Testament peace theology. In the Old Testament, "perfect" peace results from Yahweh's covenant restoration. Liberation is a realization of sociopolitical justice in eschatological salvation history.[183] Yahweh said to Moses in the wilderness of Sinai, "If you will indeed obey my voice and keep my covenant, then you shall be my own possession among the peoples, for all the earth is mine" (Exod. 19:5). The covenant was God's gracious gift to bring shalom to Israel and God 's act of love to protect them from enemies. It implies certain obligations to maintain and nourish the relationship between Yahweh and Israel.[184] God's jubilee as a part of the covenant supports a concrete performance method of visible sociopolitical justice; liberation of the captive and slave, cancellation of debts, and redistribution of land (Lev. 25, Deut. 15).

The Jubilee Message in Isaiah 61:1-3 is a Christological and eschatological declaration of the coming kingdom of God which will be held by Christ: "The spirit of the Lord God is upon me; because the Lord has anointed me to bring good news to the afflicted; he has sent me to bind up the broken-hearted,

---

[183] J.H Yoder, *Politics of Jesus*, Michigan, Willian B. Eerdmans, 2con., 1994, pp. 28-29; Ben Ollenbeger, "Peace and God's Action against Chaos in the Old Testament," *The Church's Peace Witness*, M.E. Miller and B.N. Gingerich, ed., Grand Rapids, Wm. B. Eerdamns, 1994, pp. 70-71.
[184] Perry B. Yoder, Shalom: *The Bible's Word for Salvation*, Justice and Peace, Kansas, Faith and life Press, 1987, pp. 75-82.

to proclaim liberty to captives, and freedom to prisoners…"[185] The peace of the Old Testament should be understood in the dimension of macro-restoration logic (see Figure 6).

The 'perfect' jubilee peace, which God wants, includes sociopolitical, spiritual, and eschatological restoration ideas. The religious approach to peacebuilding has been ignored by many peace scholars. Johan Galtung, a distinguished peace scholar, also recognized 'the definition of peace' as becoming a major part of a scientific strategy. In order to explain peace as the absence of structural violence he emphasized political, economic, and cultural interaction as important according to a general theory of social structure.[186] The peaceful reunification and restoration of humanity between North and South Korea should be recognized by the religious application of the Jubilee or the Sabbath year. The reunion of 10 million separated families, the return to each individual of family property, and the national redistribution of land are the needs of the times. This is according to the first Korea Jubilee year (2000).

Christ's Jubilee Theology as a Restoration of Humanity

In this part, I want to focus on the meaning of a restoration of humanity from antagonism into the love of the enemy. This is attained from the prophetic understanding of the Jubilee year. The reason is not simply because Christ's Jubilee declaration implies an evaluative analysis of political issues. Instead, Christ himself declared the coming of his kingdom as the key to

---

[185] Ulrich Mauser, *The Gospel of Peace*, Louisville, Westminster/ John Knox, 1992, p. 26; S.H. Ringe, *Jesus, Liberation, and the Biblical Jubilee*, Philadelphia, Fortress Press, 1985, pp. 33-36.
[186] Johnan Galtung, "Violence, Peace, and Peace Research," *Contemporary Peace Research*, Ghanshyam Paradesi, ed., Brighton, the Harvester Press, 1982, p. 85; *Journal of Peace Research*, Vol. 6, 1969, pp. 167-191.

solving political issues. Yoder found the Jubilee of "a visible sociopolitical, economic restructuring of relations among the people of God, achieved by intervention in the person of Jesus as the Anointed and filled with the spirit in Luke's gospel."[187] Erich Dinkler argued that "the use and meaning of 'eirene' in the various layers of the New Testament tradition and….in several early extracanonical writings (e.g. I Clement and Gregory of Nazianzus) are largely coherent with the Hebrew Scripture's use and meaning of Shalom." Willard M. Swartly also argued that "hence the New Testament peace teachings should not be restricted in meaning to nor coopted directly into contemporary political peace causes; rather, the peace experienced between God and humans in communities of faith by means of Jesus Christ must be valued as a unique achievement that in turn provides a distinctive offer of peace and reconciliation to the world."[188]

In the study of the prophetic understanding of Christ's Jubilee declaration, we should begin with Jesus' temptation (Luke 4:1-13). Jesus declares the Jubilee as a restoration of God's dominance. 4:1-13 is a prelude to 4:14-20, micro-vision.

A comparison of macro-restoration logic and micro-restoration logic toward Jubilee theology can be seen in <Figure 6>. Why did Jesus mention strong micro-restoration logic as the prophetic tool of the Jubilee vision in his first public ministry? The reason is that Jesus had already experienced macro-restoration logic through the victory against the devil before opening his prophetic public ministry. During the Jubilee years, Jesus recognized aspects of micro-restoration logic. Because Jesus knew and experienced the religious dimension of the coming kingdom of God, he knew how human life in the kingdom of God should be regulated sociologically. He also knew how the political fight against satanic power should be fought.

---

[187] John Howard Yoder, *The Politics of Jesus*, p. 32.
[188] See Willard M. Swartly, "Introducing the New Testament Essays on Eirene," *The Meaning of Peace: Biblical Studies*, edited by Perry B. Yoder and Willard M. Swartly, Westminster/ John Knox Press, 1992, pp. 152-153.

<Figure 6>   Macro-Restoration Logic

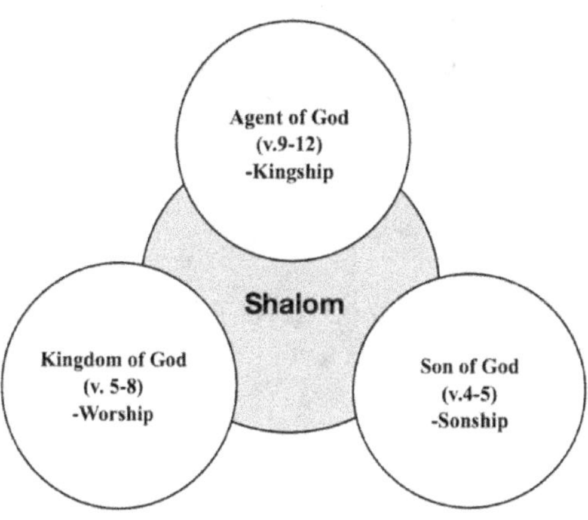

<Figure 7>   Micro-Restoration Logic

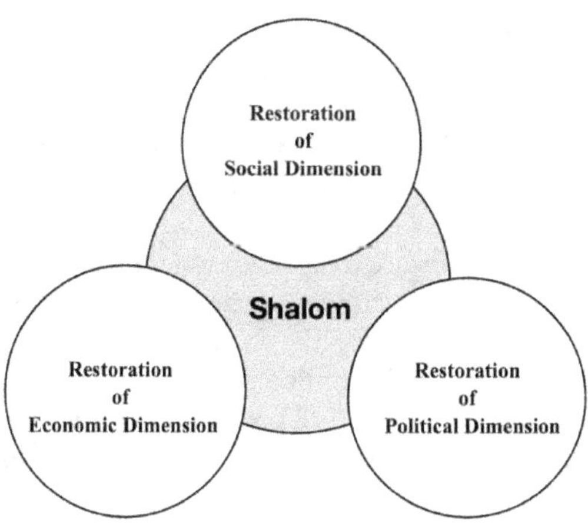

In Jesus 'macro-restoration logic, we can understand "the

work of Christ was the restoration of humanity, that is, the restoration of human beings to wholeness as a human being."[189] For this reason, through the pre-experience of Satan as an enemy in the wilderness, Jesus could strongly declare a visible sociopolitical and economic restructuring of relations among the people of God, and teach his peace theology toward how to love our enemies.

Historical Background of the Korean Jubilee Year

Appearance of Japanese Imperialism and Early Korea (Choson)

Historically, Korea's cruelest long-term antagonist was Japan. In March 1894, the so-called "Donghak Lan", a massive religious and political uprising to reform the government, developed in Korea. The Korean Government called on China for military aid.[190] This was the opportunity Japan had been looking for, to drive Chinese influence from Korea. Japan declared war on China on August 1, 1894. Chinese forces were destroyed on August 26, 1894.

On April 17, 1895, a peace treaty between the two belligerents was signed, and Korea was recognized as an independent nation.[191] On June 24, 1910, the Korean Government was compelled to sign an agreement entrusting police affairs to the Japanese. On August 22, 1910, Korea was annexed to Japan. Konzou Uchimura, a non-church movement leader, lamented

---

[189] C. Norman Kraus, *The Healing Christ: Social Services and The Evangelical Mission*, PA, Herald Press, 1972, p. 34.

[190] Japan made an attempt to eliminate Chinese influence by military means from 1824.

[191] Chung, Kyung-Cho, *Korea Tomorrow*, New York, Macmillan, 1956, p. 158.

Korea's nationhood loss. But many Japanese church leaders welcomed the forced annexation of Korea.[192]

<Table 12>   Damages Suffered by Korea Insurgents

Period	Killed	Wounded	Captured	Total	Guns	Daggers	Spears
1907 (Aug.-Dec.)	3,627	1,492	139	5,258	1235	7	0
1908	11,562	1,719	1,417	14, 698	508	85	59
1909	2,374	435	329	3,138	1,392	248	18
1910	125	54	48	227	116	20	1
1911	9	6	61	76	10	1	0
TOTAL	**17,697**	**3,706**	**1,994**	**23,397**	**3,261**	**361**	**78**

Source: Headquarters, Japanese *Garrison Army in Korea*, Boto Tobatsushi [Record of Subjugation of Insurgents], Seoul, 1913.

Soon after the annexation individual liberty became non-existent. The Japanese controlled all political, economic, and religious activity. Worship meetings cannot be held without permission. Free speech was abolished. Koreans could not publish newspapers or magazines freely. Names of towns and even personal names were changed to Japanese. From 1907 to 1011, the Korean people fought against the Japanese for their rights restoration. However, this resistance resulted in many deaths or captures by Japanese troops. One can see the scale of their real action in <Table 12>.

Korea's protest against the Japanese reached a climax on March 1, 1919. Five thousand people attended Pagoda Park in Seoul. As soon as the introductory statement of Korea's Declaration of Independence was read by a young student, the

---

[192] Ken J. Shenk, "The Church in Japan faces Militarism and Violence: A historical study," *The Role of Church in Society*, Urbane Peachey, ed., International Mennonite Peace Committee, 1988, p. 93. Oh, Yun-Tae, *Nikan Kirisutokoyo Koryushi (History of Christian Reconciliation between Japan and Korea)*, Tokyo, 1968, p. 122.

crowd echoed the cry of 'Manse!' [193] and displayed the Korean flag. The streets were filled with people shouting for Korea's independence. The Japanese police dispersed the crowd.[194]

<Table 13>   Religious Affiliation of the Arrested

Denomination	Male	Female	Total
Chondogyo	2,268	15	2,283
Shichongyo	14	0	14
Buddhist	220	0	220
Confucians	346	0	346
Methodist	518	42	560
Presbyterian	2,254	232	2,486
Congregational	7	0	7
Other Protestants	286	34	320
Catholics	54	1	55
Other religions	21	0	21
No religious affiliation	9,255	49	9,304
Unknown	3,809	98	3,907
TOTAL	**19,052**	**439**	**19,523**

Source: It is quoted from Lee, *Korean Nationalism*, p. 115.

For the period from March 1 to April 30, 1919, the statistics of the Japanese gendarmerie show 848 incidents, 357 incidents prevented, an ally of 587,641 persons involved and arrests of

---

[193] Manse means "Long live Korea!"
[194] Lee, Chong-Sik, *the Politics of Korean Nationalism*, Berkeley and Los Angeles, University of California Press, 1963, p. 81.

26,713 persons.[195] But by the statistics from nationalist sources, for the period from March 1, 1919 to March 1, 1920, 7,645 Koreans were killed and 45,562 were injured.[196] Religious groups sponsored the independence movement and they resisted strongly against the Japanese troops through various nonviolent or violent actions. The Korean governor-general estimates the religious affiliation of those arrested as shown in <Table 13>.

Soon after the Declaration of Independence, Dr. Rhee Syng-Man established the Provisional Government in Shanghai's French concession during the winter of 1919. On December 1, 1943, President Franklin D. Roosevelt, Generalissimo Chiang Kai-Shek, and Prime Minister Winston Churchill declared that 'in due course' Korea should become free and independent. With Japan's surrender on August 15, 1945, Japanese colonial rule of 36 years ended.

The Korean War and National Division

On August 15, 1948, Dr. Rhee Syng-Man became the first President of the Republic of Korea (ROK). Three weeks later on September 10, 1948, Kim Il-Sung also became the Premier of the Democratic People's Republic of Korea (DPRK) in North Korea. But the conflict between the Soviet Union and the United States continued after the establishment of the United Nations Commission on Korea. Military support from both the Soviet Union and the United States led to hostility between North and South Korea.

On June 25, 1950, North Korea invaded South Korea with Soviet Union help. Although the Korean War ended on August 8, 1953, the war result was extraordinary. During the Korean War the communists (North Korea and the Soviet Union) persecuted Christians in a similar way to the Japanese. The total

---

[195] Ibid., p. 113.
[196] Ibid., p. 114.

Christian casualties were estimated to be 408; the captured church leaders were about 50, and the destroyed churches 1,373. Catholic Church leaders were also persecuted. Their total casualties and captured church leaders were 150, and 98 were foreign missionaries.

The persecutions by the Japanese and the communists were a combination of political and sociological, as well as, a religious hostility. As a result, this antagonism should be resolved for the 'third jubilee' to take place on June 25, 2050. It is also a task of the mission toward peaceful Korean reunification. The role of religious groups in the nationalistic movement against Japanese colonialism and communism was significant. Peace theology should help modern Korean Christianity and other religious groups reconcile Korea-Japan conflicts and Korea-North Korean conflicts.

The Restoration Logic of Peace according to Korea's Jubilee

Religious Restoration

As soon as Japanese imperialism ended, North and South Korean churches started rebuilding churches. They reformed the church's faith and institutions such as Hezekiah (2 King. 29) and Josiah (2 Chron. 34). Pyongyang, the capital of North Korea was a mission center for Korean Christianity. At that time, North Korea had many Christians (about 300,000-350,000) and churches (about 2,000). Christianity in North Korea accounts for 3 percent of the total population (9,400,000). In South Korea, Christians number 100,000 with 200 churches.[197] Korea's

---

[197] Kim, Yong-Bok, "Kookgaboondan kwa Kidokkyojokdaeung" (Nation Division and Christian Attitude) *Korean Church as a Peace-maker*, Society Board of the Korean Presbyterian General Assembly, 1986, p.113.

first Bible school was Pyongyang Theological Seminary.

North Korean churches established The Five Providence's United Church of North Korea. IN December 1945 Jang Dae Hyun Presbyterian Church was established in Pyongyang.[198] They decided to consecrate the faith of the church's leaders and reform the church's institutions stained from Japanese religion. The South Korean churches started the reconstruction movement according to each denomination (Methodist-January 14, 1946; Presbyterian-June, 1946; Sanctification church-September 10, 1945; Salvation Army-October, 1946; Baptist-February 9, 1946).[199] However, with the beginning of the Korean War, Korean churches were persecuted again, especially by the communists, North Korea and the Soviet Union. Many North Korean churches were killed because of their faith in communism's dictates. The number of Christian leaders persecuted was as follows: Presbyterian (177), Methodist (44) and Sanctification Church (11).[200] Because of that repression, today in the second jubilee year North Korea has several public churches including Bongsoo Church, Chilgok Church, and several house churches.

According to the International Religious Freedom Report 2005 conducted by the U.S. Department of State and released by the Bureau of Democracy, Human Rights, and Labor, North Korea's "number of religious believers is unknown but estimated by the Government to be 10,000 Protestants, 10,000 Buddhists, and 4,000 Catholics." Estimates by South Korean church-related groups are considerably higher. In addition, the Chondogyo Young Friends Party, a government-approved group based on a traditional religious movement, has approximately 40,000 practitioners. They also have the Chosun Christian Alliance and the Pyongyang Theological Academy.

But we should recognize some significant historical meanings, which justify Korea's religious Jubilee. This is the restoration of spiritual traditions in North Korea. This was a cause of the

---

[198] Ibid., pp. 106-107.
[199] Ibid., p. 108.
[200] Ibid., p. 121.

revival of early Korean Christianity in the Holy Land or early Korean Christianity. It is a religious restoration of Christianity in North Korea as a result of the martyr faith of early Korean Christianity. Thirdly, it is a restoration and religious liberation for the Catacomb faith of underground church believers. By an unofficial report, the first generation who experienced Christianity's martyr faith are still keeping their faith in underground churches in secret.

Geo-economic Restoration

The problem of land is a very important factor for economic justice of Jubilee theology. According to Israel tradition, ancient Near East land tenure regulations set limits on individuals' rights to buy and sell land at will. This concept of an inalienable land is based on the Hebrew Jubilee.[201] Traditionally, the land of Israel was divided according to the families in the clan, and the families received equal shares of the land by allotment as the basic economic unit.[202] Land is very important as a theological factor as well as an economic factor. Yahweh gave peace to the land (Lev. 26:6). Therefore, the loss of their land implies the destruction of the temple, the end of the David dynasty, the loss of their nationhood, the apparent invalidation of the Sinai covenant, the decimation of the priesthood and the end of sacrifice.[203]

Geo-economically the main elements of Korea's national economy were the land and the people. Korean economy, however, was apportioned to Japan's economy under Japanese imperialism. Korean farmers were dispossessed and their land was turned over to Japanese immigrants on an easy purchase plan. This forced about two million Koreans off their land. Of

---

[201] Jeffery A. Fager, *Land Tenure and the Biblical Jubilee*, Sheffield, JSOT Press, 1993, p.27.
[202] Ibid., p.28.
[203] Ibid., p. 42; R.W. Klein, *Israel in Exile: A Theological Interpretation*, Overtures to Biblical Theology, Philadelphia, Fortress, 1979, pp. 3-5.

the 250 million bushels of rice produced annually, 45 percent are exported to Japan. For this reason, the Korean people starved, and Japan developed Korea as a source of raw materials for its own industries, using it as a dumping ground for surplus industrial products.

The Korean War reduced the national economy. J.H. Shoemaker divided Korea's postwar economic elements into four dimensions: (1) the land (area topography, climate, mineral and power resources); (2) the people (population and characteristics); (3) technical ability (capacity for production); (4) relations with other countries (power and trade position in relation to other nations of the world).[204] However during the Korean War, roads transportation facilities, communication systems, factories, mines, and irrigation canals were destroyed. The main reason for economic inflation was the combination of normal revenue sources and vast military expenditures.

The economic growth or North Korea has decreased and many people are in difficulty because of a serious food shortage. In addition, they have spent much money, time, and labor on the military. In 1991, North Korea's defense expenditure was 24 percent of its GNP. 1990 GNP was $29 billion. South Korea's 1990 GNP was $238 billion; 1991 defense expenditure was 4.5 percent. South Korea should try to restore inter-Korean economic cooperation in the spirit of the Jubilee year. This does not mean unifying the country by absorbing North Korea. We have already witnessed the experience of West Germany; the integration would certainly bankrupt the Republic. Therefore, both Koreas should restore inter-Korean economic cooperation based on the Agreement of Reconciliation and Non-aggression.

Political Restoration

The declaration of a political Jubilee as liberation is a climax

---

[204] J.H. Shoemaker, *Notes on Korea's Postwar Economic Position*, New York, I.P.R., 1947, p.1

for the people, much more than the cancellation of debts and the return of lost land. It is the emancipation of slaves and the captured. In the case of the captured or enslaved, it is proper to release them in the Jubilee year. Yahweh emphasizes shalom before war against enemies; "you shall offer it terms of peace" (Deut. 20:10). Benjamin's tribe is finally reconciled by a proclamation of peace (Judges 21:13).

However, Korea lost 20,000,000 people, 300,000 Christians and many orphans and widows in the Korean War. Political restoration between North and South Korea is our last task. But there are many obstacles to reunification.

First, ideological opinions on South Korea's anti-communist ideology are almost polarized. The different ideologies and socio-political structures form the antagonism between North and South Korea. Mori Yoshinov divided anti-communist ideology into periods as follows: a) Anti-Bolshevism: August-September 1945; US Army Forces versus Anti-Communist Forces: September- December 1945; c) Birth of Anti-Communist Ideology: December 1945- June 1946; and d) Post-Civil War: June 1950.[205]

Second, the antagonism is an exclusive communication channel between North and South Korea without forgiveness and reconciliation. Jong-Bok Lee divided structural relations between North and South Korea as follows: a) Hostility and War: 1948-1971; b) Communications Relationship: 1971-1973; Antagonistic Relationship: 1973- 1984; and d) Communications Restoration: 1984- Present.[206] He emphasized the necessity of reconciliation without tension between North and South Korea.

A third obstacle is the necessity of developing an ideology to harmonize with communist doctrines (the Juche ideology of Kim II Sung). Conflicting factors formed between communism and capitalism in Korea: collectivism versus individualism, ethnocentrism versus internationalism, spiritual determinism

---

[205] Mori Yoshinov,"The Formation of Korea Anti-nationalism," *Korea and International Politics*, Seoul, Institute of Far East Asian Studies, 1989 Vol. 5, No.2, pp. 171-192.
[206] Ibid., pp. 123-149.

versus material determinism. It is also a conflict between the 'Juche' ideology or Marxism and Christianity.

The enemy recognition, according to the anti-communistic movement and its antagonistic political relations, is divided into positive and negative types. Generally, the post-war generation and students who were influenced by the Juche ideology, have a favorable (or liberal) perspective towards North Korea's many wrongdoings. Those with a positive outlook have decreased in number.

In any case, we should recognize that Korean reunification is the most significant national task for the restoration of a common community of unity. Both countries need mutual confidence and tolerance, especially since Kim Il-Sung's death and North Korea's economic difficulty. They cannot solve their serious food shortage. It is important for South Korea to regard North Korea as our homogeneous blood relatives, but as aggressive communists. The government should also take a more positive stance, a peace agreement based on anti-war and anti-nuclear weapons in the Korean peninsula.

Therefore, Korean Christianity should study Jubilee theology as a political restoration. The aim is to support the Korean political jubilee by exhibiting Christ's spirit of reconciliation and nonviolence. Jesus' second commandment was "Love your neighbor as yourself" (Matt. 22:39). Love is "a proper participation with other persons whose commitments are not the same as ours, whose priorities are not the same as ours."[207]

We should study the keys to problem solving toward our conflicts according to the biblical and scientific method. It is very important to compare this antagonism to that of the synoptic Gospels, according to personal, interpersonal, and group antagonistic dimensions.

---

[207] Myron S. Augsburger, "Nonviolence as a Life-Style," *Perspectives on Peacemaking: Biblical Options in the Nuclear Age*, edited by Jon A. Bembaum, California, Regal Books, 1984, pp. 152-153; See Myron S. Augsburger & Dean C. Curry, *Nuclear Arms: Two Views on World Peace*, Texas, Word Books, 1987, pp. 49-53, 55-56.

The Restoration of Humanity toward the Enemy according to the Synoptic Gospels Personal Antagonism

Historically, because of Japanese colonialism and Marxist-Leninist Communism, many Korean people have unconditional personal antagonism against them. They dislike Japan and communist countries, and their xenophobia makes them hatable enemies. They fundamentally dislike the humanity of the Japanese and communists, as well as their wrongdoing.

According to the Synoptic Gospels, Jesus also experienced various personal antagonistic relationships as <Table 14>. In Luke 8:29-39 the demonic showed their hatred towards Jesus with hatred as soon as they saw him. The case is the same for the man possessed by an unclean demon in Luke 4:31-37. The love of Christ manifested itself as problem solving towards them in the form of healing accompanied by salvation. In Luke 8:35, the demon-possessed man healed by Jesus sat at his feet. From Christ 's birth, there was political antagonism against Him. Herod the King gated Christ. Herod's antagonism was a political conflict of kingship (Matt.2:2). Similar to this, those with personal animosity can develop a satanic hatred. The Jew also had a strong antagonism against enemies and Gentiles (Luke 15:1-2; 16:14; John 4:9)

Today such an example of personal antagonism, based on national conflict exists in the two Koreas. Those North Korean people who were ideologized by Marxist Engelism and "Juche Thought" (social communism by Kim II Sung) have a basic personal antagonism towards South Korea and the U.S.A. <Table 14>. Christ's way of problem solving towards the enemy is forgiveness, healing and salvation based on his love. Therefore, the personal antagonism of the North, and South Korea, should be resolved by Messianic shalom with unconditional love. This is more than secularized social and political institutions.

<Table 14>   Christ's Conflict and Resolution

Type	Enemy	Text	Issues	Christ's Resolution
Personal antagonism relation	1. A man possessed by the spirit of unclean demon	Luke 4:31-37	Demoniac condemnation to Jesus	Healing
	2. The demoniac	Luke 8:26-39	Demoniac hatred to Jesus	Healing & Salvation (v.35)
	3. Herod the King	Matthew 2	Political hatred to Jesus	Appearance of angel of the Lord as of the third way (v.13)
Inter-personal relation	1. Jesus/Jews	John 10:22-39	The problem of Jesus' deity	Messianic teaching of faith (v.38)
	2. Jesus/ Samaritan Woman	John 4:7-42	Historical Hostility (v.9)	Messianic teaching of an eternal life, and koinonia (v.14, v.26)
Triangle antagonism relation	1. Jesus/Jews/ Adulterous woman	John 8:3-11	Adultery and Law	Messianic forgiveness (v.7)
	2. Jesus/ enemies- priest, elder, officers/ Peter	Luke 22:47-53 Matthew 26:47-51 John 13:1-11	Judas' bargain	Messianic forgiveness and healing (v.51)
	3. Lord/slave- 10,000 talent)/ slave- 100 denarii	Matthew 18:23-34	Forgiveness of debt	Messianic parable of forgiveness and economic justice
	4. Jesus/ruler/ soldiers	Luke 23:26-38	Mocking and rebuking Jesus	Messianic forgiveness and love (v.34)

As Paul says, our enemies need spiritual healing of their antagonism. It is very significant for them. "Our struggle is not against flesh and blood, but against the rulers, the powers, against the world forces of this darkness, against the spiritual forces of wickedness in the heavenly places" (Ephesians 6:12).

Interpersonal Antagonism

While Japanese colonialism against early Korea (Choson) was over imperialistic dominance, the Communist invasion was an ideological war against South Korea related to the hegemony battle between the Soviet Union and the United States. People before the Korean War did not understand the difference between communism ideology, and they fought and killed one another. Therefore, ideology separated our families, society, and nation into the left and the right wing. This interpersonal antagonism in Korea has remained unchanged until now.

<Table 15>　　Instruction Idea of the North Korean Labor Party

Time	Idea Tradition
North Korea Labor Party foundation (1948.6)	Marx-Leninism
The Second Campaign Labor Party (1948.3)	Marx-Leninism
N.K.and S.K. Labor party Joint Campaign (1948.6)	Marx-Leninism
The Third Campaign(1956.4)	Marx-Leninism and Though of Korea Revolution
The Fourth Campaign(1961.9)	Marx-Leninism and Thought of Korea Revolution and Thought of Revolution against Japan and Kim Il Sung's Juche Ideology
The Fifth Campaign (1970.11)	Marx-Leninism and Kim Il Sung's Juche Ideology
The Sixth Campaign(1980.10)	**Kim Il Sung's Juche Ideology**

Source: Korean National Unification Board, *Introduction of North Korea*, Seoul: Korea National Unification Board, 1983, P.27

Jesus was also faced with interpersonal hostility. John 10:22-39 shows this conflict was very serious. "The Jews took up stones against him to stone him." The Jews were antagonistic toward Jesus because of his claims to be deity. "For a good work we do not stone You, but for blasphemy; and because You, being a man, make Yourself out to be God (33 v.) Although Jesus did not say "Yes" he identified himself as part of God's genealogy indirectly, by explaining about almighty God. By demonstrating his clear identity and generous understanding of their faith absence, Jesus ended antagonistic relations with Jews. John 10:22-39 is a passive event, but 4:7-42 is an active event. The reason for this is that Jews have no dealings with Samaritans. Jesus touched on the problem of historical conflict (hostility) himself. In this text, Jesus shows us an excellent example of reconciliation through the Samaritan woman. He thought of eternal life for her, and declared himself the Messiah.

It is important for us to have an active (positive) behavior to make reconciliation, discipleship, and fellowship as the restoration of humanity with our enemies. Therefore, Korean Christianity should take the initiative in eliminating the sense of economic and ideological superiority, as well as the exclusivism of communism.

Group-Dimension Antagonism

The Korean people have complicated hostility. Korea has experienced sociopolitical antagonistic relations with many countries in the international dimension, like Japan, China, the Soviet Union, North Korea, and the United States. Korea has acted in accordance with the interests of big powers. However, whether in the personal or national dimension, we should have broad patience to resolve group antagonism.

Jesus Shows us a generous mind, forgiveness, and love of enemy in triangular antagonistic relations. According to John 8:3-11, Jesus was involved in a triangular conflict between Jews and an adulterous woman. Jesus said, "He who is without sin among you, let him be the first to throw a stone at me" (11:v). This order is a declaration of Messianic love against the social Roman Law, and the religious Mosaic Law. And, it is also a revolutionary declaration of a Messianic Jubilee, namely a macro-political or eschatological event, Christ's nonviolent revolution of love, and the Messianic Kingdom of God.

In Luke 22:47-53, Jesus is faced with a political triangle (or square) relationship. All of us can assume that this is a very serious situation. The characters are as follows: "the multitude"

(47 v.) --a group of Roman cohorts and officers sent by the Chief Priests and the Pharisees (John 18:3), Judas, Simon Peter with a sword (John 18:10), and Jesus. In his excitement, Peter struck the high priest's slave (Malchus, John 18:10), and cut off his right ear. Peter might have aimed at Judas instead of Malchus. Jesus sublimated this political event to macro-restoration logic. Considering this event to be the 'second significant eschatological forgiveness', I would like to call it one of the greatest. The first eschatological forgiveness occurs in the case of an adulterous woman in John 8:3-11. Eschatological forgiveness means salvation. As Norman Kraus mentioned, salvation is in process-a movement toward a good, which will be reached in the eschaton (the end or consummation).[208]

Jesus ordered strongly, "Stop! No more of this" (51 v.). It means "suffer ye thus far"-K.J.V. Jesus did not focus on only Peter 's act. It is a declaration of visible political forgiveness for Judas as an enemy. Second, it is a healing through the power of the Son of God, and a healing through political justice. Third, it is a declaration of visible macro-political forgiveness against darkness disturbing the coming God's kingdom.

Matthew 18:23-34 helps us understand messianic forgiveness through his parable. In this text the characters are the King (Lord) and two slaves. A certain King's "top-to-bottom forgiveness" of the debt between the one who owed the thousand talents and the fellow slave who owed a hundred denarii means unconditional Messianic forgiveness by the power as son of God, and forgiveness as an action of economic justice toward the poor. Because 'top-to-bottom forgiveness' implies an order (like God-Christ-people of God), it is proper to love our enemies. Jesus used this principle in his prayer: "remit us our debts as we ourselves have remitted their debts" (Matt. 6:12). The verb "aphiemi" means "remit" or "forgive a debt". This meaning is the same as the verb "forgive" of paraptoma (transgression) in 14v.-15v.: "For if you forgive men for their

---

[208] C. Norman Kraus, *The Healing Christ: Social Services and The Evangelical Mission*, p. 32.

transgressions, your heavenly Father will also forgive you: but if you do not forgive men, then your Father will not forgive your transgressions." The verb "aphieme" or the noun form of the same verb "aphesis" used regularly in connection with the jubilee (e.g.Lev.25:28, 54; Deut. 15:1ff.; Isa.61:2; Jer.35:8).[209]

Finally, in Luke 23:26-43, Jesus faces the climax of a triangular antagonistic relationship. The triangle relationship's actors in this event are rulers who sneered, soldiers who mocked Jesus (v.35-36), and the criminal who hurled abuse (v.39). In this context, Jesus shows a panorama of eschatological forgiveness, love, salvation, and resurrection. I want to call this forgiveness (v.34.) the third most powerful macro-political forgiveness. This is not simply compassion for enemies, but an act of forgiveness brought on by a messianic love revolution. Messianic love of the enemy is connected with his eschatological salvation and resurrection event. In order to show this, Jesus forgave the criminal directly, and gave him citizenship in God's Kingdom. Rather than simply humanistic reconciliation, love of enemy means eschatological salvation and eschatological resurrection.

Jesus' forgiveness of the enemy means an unconditional love as a nonviolent revolution, salvation as a messianic mission, and eschatological resurrection as the coming Kingdom of God. Therefore, Korean Christianity should take the initiative to forgive our enemies, including Japanese and North Koreans.

Conclusion

Korea (Choson) as a peace-loving country has experienced many kinds of conflicts under the persecution of Japanese colonialists and the violent ideologization by the communists (North Korea including China, the Soviet Union). Korean Christianity has resisted them violently and nonviolently, in the

---

[209] John Howard Yoder, *The Politics of Jesus*, p.6. See footnote no. 5.

name of 'Just War'. Of course, we fought against many kinds of conflicts through positive non-violent revolution through the Independence Movement (1918), Anti-trusteeship Movement (1945), etc.

Despite these actions, Korea has not reunified. Korean Christian churches should declare the Korean Jubilee based on Messianic macro-political forgiveness towards the enemy. It is not forgiveness that comes from human nature, but from God. God is the one who has authority over war and judgment against the enemy, not us. In Romans 12:14, 17-19 Paul writes, "Bless those who persecute you; bless and do not curse." Do not repay anyone evil for evil.... If it is possible, live at peace with everyone. Do not revenge, my friends. Jesus said "Bless those who curse you, pray for those who mistreat you (Luke 6:28)." The non-repayment of evil is one of Christianity's basic principles. In Romans 12:10-13, Paul states "Some of the good things we are to cling to brotherly affection, mutual honor, zealous service, joyful and patient hope, and generous hospitality."[210] Therefore, Christian churches take the initiative in developing anti-war, anti-nuclear weapons, and anti-military culturalism based on the basic principles of Christianity.

Christ gave us eschatological forgiveness for the enemy. It is a spiritual power that sublimates the power of darkness into Messianic love and leads our enemies to salvation. Christ's unconditional messianic forgiveness is a peaceful tool eliminating antagonistic relationships against our enemies. It is also a graceful gift increasing humanity's restoration toward peaceful Korean reunification.

The church's participation in the reconciliation between North and South Korea needs to be an ecumenical movement based on 'shalom' in the Old Testament and 'eireine' in the New Testament. Neither is it individual or denominational, nor is it exclusive to Marxist or Niebuhrian worldviews. It is better to participate through interdenominational or inter-Christian

---

[210] John R.W. Stott, "Christian Responses to Good and Evil: A Study of Romans 12: 9-13: 10," *Perspectives on Peace Making: Biblical Options in the Nuclear Age*, pp.43-56.

NGO institutions because it needs "the pacifism of the messianic community experiencing in this shared life a foretaste of God's Kingdom."[211] The Messianic peace movement based on Christ's forgiveness and love in the Korean peninsula will be a cornerstone of macro-Asian forgiveness, and it will have a significant role for the world-reconciliation and peace movement in the post-cold war era.

When Korean peaceful reunification is realized through the Korean Jubilee, based on 'shalom' of the Old Testament and 'eirene' of the New Testament, it will become a global movement. The reasons are as follows: First, Korean peaceful reunification will encourage Asia's evangelization. North Korea is a unique country where missionaries cannot enter with the Gospel. Second, Korea's peaceful reunification will end social communist ideology. While North Korea has not opened China as a social communist country, it is opening to other countries. Finally, the peaceful reunification of Korea will end a nation-dividing conflict. I hope Korea will someday be a peace-leading country in the world. And, I am sure Korean Christianity will be a peace mission-leading group in Asia in the future, like the Mennonite Church in the World.

---

[211] John Howard Yoder, *Nevertheless*, p. 135.

128

6

SOCIO-POLITICAL CHANGE AND DEVELOPMENT OF THE NONVIOLENCE MOVEMENT IN ASIA OF THE TWENTIETH CENTURY

130

Socio-political Change and Development of the Nonviolence Movement in Asia of the Twentieth Century

After World War I, through the industrial revolution, monopolistic capitalism was formed and profit rates decreased in Russia. For this reason, the uprising of the peasants against feudal lords and feudalism and the revolution of the workers against the exploitation of the industrial proletariat happened in 1905 and 1917. In late 1918 as soon as the American president, Woodrow Wilson, proclaimed "Fourteen Points," which was the spirit of self-determination as a new foreign policy, the Korean people hoped to restore their lost sovereignty through the independence movement against Japanese colonial rule, and thousands of Korean people took a nationwide movement in Asia. Two Asian nonviolent movements were affected by it: Gandhi's Satyagraha Campaign and the Chinese May Fourth Movement. On April 6, 1919, one month after the Korean March First Movement began, a nationwide Satyagraha Campaign against the Rowlatt Bills was led by Gandhi in India. In Nehru's letter to his daughter, which was written in prison and contained a rambling account of history for young people, he emphasized young students' participation in the Korean March First Movement to his daughter.

For many years the struggle for independence continued and there were many outbreaks, the most important being in 1919. Korea's people, especially young men and women, struggled gallantly against tremendous odds. An organization fighting for freedom once declared independence, and thus deified them for their actions! Thus, deliberately they sacrificed themselves for their ideals.... You will be interested to know that young Korean girls, many of them fresh from college, played a prominent part in the struggle.[212]

On May 4, 1919, two months after the March First Movement, patriotic students in Peking protested the Versailles Peace Conference decision that Japan should retain defeated Germany's rights and possessions in Shantung. Many of them were arrested. Protest waves spread throughout China's major cities. By the students' protest, the government released the arrested students and refuse to sign the Versailles Treaty. Zhou En Lai mentioned, "The Chinese May Fourth Movement happened because of the awakening of the Korean March First Movement," in the preface of publication for the 'The Chongging Student Union Newspaper' on July 1919. [213] A famous leader of the neo-culture movement in China, Cheung Du Xiu, praised the Korean March First Movement and appealed to follow it to students and Christianity:

> The recent Korean independence movement was admirable, honest and heroic. The people behind this movement believe that weapons shouldn't be used accurately. They accomplished a new era in revolution history.... We cannot avoid shame when comparing ourselves to the Korean people. Students and Christians made up the majority of the participants in the Korean independence movement. So let us stop looking down on Christians and recognize the need to increase education development. Students and Christians of

---

[212] Jawahartal Nehru, *Glimpses of World History*, 4th eds., New York: John Day Company, 1942, p. 465.

[213] Huai Si, ed., *The poems and letters' Collections of the Premier Zhou's Youth*, Vol. 1, Sichuam People Publication Co., 1979, p.149, quoted from *Keun Dae Choson Ui Sahoi Wa SaSang (A Society and Thoughts of Recent Korea)*, edited by Kang Chae-On, Korean version, Seoul: Baiksan Seadang, 1983, p.57.

China, let us awaken from our sleep![214]

On March 23, 1919, the Peking University students in their literary coterie magazine, Xin Chao (New Trend), mentioned that the Korean independence movement gave three great instructions for all revolutions in the future: Revolution of Nonviolence Movement, Revolution of Challenge against Impossibility, and Revolution by Pure Students.[215] Although the Korean independence movement gave some effectiveness towards the Indian and Chinese nonviolence movements, I would like to conduct a comparative study of the Korean and Indian movements because both were the Asian gospel of nationwide nonviolent movements as well as the independence movements under colonial rule.

Social Structure and Change under Colonial Rule

Unlike the Chinese May Fourth Movement by nationalists and students against Japanese troops, the Korean and Indian independence movements were full-scale protests. Under British and Japanese colonial rule, both countries had internal contradictions in their social structures and interstate political conflicts. Koreans encountered traditional social conflicts between peasants and feudal lords. Twenty thousand Korean peasants tried to demand the reformation of economic and social contradictions through the Tonghak movement in May of 1894. This was called a peasants' revolution. Due to its failure, those contradictions continued until Japan's annexation. However, under Japanese colonial rule, both the feudal lords and

---

[214] Cheung Du Xiu, "Feelings of the Korean Independence Movement," *Weekly Review*, No. 14, March 23, 1919. I translated this part from *A Society and Thoughts of Recent Korea*, Korean version, edited by Kang Chae-On.
[215] Fu Yue Cheng, *The Records of Fu Zheng's Students*, Korean version, Bibliography Literature Co., 1969, p. 14, quoted from *A Society and Thoughts of Recent Korea*, edited by Kang Chae-On.

the peasants' properties and social status were exploited. Between Japanese landlords and Korean tenants, 6,502 conflicts occurred between 1933 and 1936.

Under British colonial rule, India's indigenous handicraft industries were distrusted due to the enforcement of the heavy industry of the exploitation of raw materials and labors. India's social structure, based on Hinduism and Islam had many traditional institutional contradictions. Gandhi continued to fight for the rights of the lowest Hindu caste, the untouchables, who renounced the Harijan (Children of God), miners, factory workers and poor peasants. In contrast, approximately 90% of India's population (over 300,000,000 in 1920) who depended directly on agriculture experienced the most severe famine. According to colonial powers' exploitation policies, India's and Korea's labor populations increased rapidly. They suffered physical and spiritual abuse due to the bad conditions of salary and time, which was the main reason for a labor dispute. In Korea's case, 9,111 people participated in 84 conflicts during 1919. Both countries exploited their political functions under colonial rule.[216] Indian National Congress (INC), founded in 1885, continued its activity under British colonial rule. The revised British policy announced in 1917 accepted India's self-governing institutions, though its power was limited by this policy.[217] In the case of Korea, the political situation was different. Through Japan's annexation, the Korean government was deprived of political functions, the Korean army was disbanded, and the Korean King, Emperor Kojung, was abdicated. In response, nationalists established the Korean Provisional Government in April 1919 in China to liberate Korea from Japan.

---

[216] Sung Kyung-Dae, "Korean Labors' Activity in the March First Movement," *Hankuk Keundae Saron (A Discourse on Recent Korean History)*, Vol. II Korean version, edited by Shin Young-Ha, An Byoung-Gik, and Yoon Byong-Wook, Seoul, JiSung Co., 1979, p.198.
[217] Peter Ackerman and Christopher Kruegler, *Strategic Nonviolent Conflict: The Dynamics of People Power in the Twentieth Century*, Westport Praeger, 1994, p.163.

Formation and Change Process of People Power in the Anti-colonialism Movement

One of the most remarkable similarities with both anti-colonialism movements was that they were started by the nationalistic elite group or the capitalistic leading class. One of the most remarkable differences of both movements was that Korea's leading system was gradually replaced by the middle and lower classes after the arrest of the upper class by Japanese troops while India's leading system remained unchanged. In 1885, the Indian National Congress held its first meeting in Bombay on December 28-30, establishing the nationalist movement of India. [218] The INC consisted of over 73 representatives, including ten unofficial delegates, from every province of British India. Fifty-four of the representatives were Hindu and only two were Muslim, while the remainder was mostly Parsi and Jaina. The Hindu delegates were Brahmins, more than half lawyers and the remainder journalists, land owners and scholars. Korea's leading class members of the anti-colonialism movements also consisted of nationalistic elites and religious leaders. Of the forty-nine delegates, twenty-five were Christian, nineteen were Chondogyo, two were Buddhists, and the remainder were of various other religions.[219]

At the start of the Korean March First Movement, all the upper-class people of the first stage of the leading class were arrested. The middle class took up the independence movement leadership system. They consisted of two kinds of groups: the medium and small traders, manufacturers, and landowners of the economic middle class and the new intelligent leaders of the religious sub-structure, teachers and scholars of the social

---

[218] Sir Verney Lovett, *A History of the Indian Nationalist Movement,* New York: Augustus M. Kelly Publishers, 1969, p.35.
[219] Chondogyo is the later form of Tonghak which was anti-foreign and nationalistic from the beginning.

middle class.[220] Unlike Korea, India's leading class remained constant after the Satyagraha movement and the Amritsar Massacre in 1919. At that time, India had religious conflicts throughout its regions due to elections in Bengal, Bombay, and the United Provinces. Gandhi called upon the INC to boycott the elections to usher in diarchy. During the 1920's, Gandhi united Muslims and Hindus to form the INC and nationalistic religious leaders against British colonialism.

<Table 15>   The Movement Process by the Leading Class

Nation	First Stage	Second Stage	Third Stage
India	Leading class: Congressmen	Congressmen and religious nationalists (Hindu-Muslem)	Continued
	Class: Upper class ➤	Upper and middle class ➤	Continued
Korea	Leading class: 49 representatives	Nationalists and religious leaders (Christianity, Chondogyo, and Buddhism)	Grass-roots and students centered
	Class: Upper class ➤	Middle class ➤	Lower class centered

According to <Table 15>, while India's leading class remained constant in its third period, Korea's second stage leading class was changed into the third stage leading class of lower-class people. A large group of students joined the lower class, resulting in a majority that weakened the middle-class leadership. Under Japan's cruel colonialism, the third stage leading class recognized that no compromise could be reached and a stronger protest was necessary. Unlike India's national movements, not all of Korea's movements were nonviolent. Upon the rise of the third stage, some national movements resorted to violent movements.

---

[220] Lyu Chung-Ha, "A Historical Character of The March First Movement," *A Recent Korean History of National Movements,* p.465-467.

Violence and Nonviolence in the Anti-colonialism Movement

The Korean government tried to liberate itself from Japanese colonial rule without resorting to violence. Of course, Korean soldiers and Japanese soldiers sometimes clashed, including small-scale violent actions. King Kojong decided to develop international opinions about the illegal Japanese colonial rule in Korea. He sent several governmental special agents to advocate for this to The Hague Peace Conference of 1907 in the Netherlands. King Kojong thought that the Hague Peace Conference could act as a mediator in his disputes with Japanese government.

The conference of 1907, though first proposed by U.S. President Theodore Roosevelt, was officially convened by Nicholas II. This conference sat from June 15 to Oct. 18, 1907, and was attended by 44 states. Unfortunately, although the Korean agents appealed to the foreign delegates, American, English, and Japanese delegates rejected the Korean Government's appeal in the Hague Peace Conference. Due to this issue, the Japanese government removed King Kojong from power, and forced Korean forces to disorganize. Due to the international colonial empires, King Kojong's plan to have an international mediator help solve this problem failed.

Very interesting is that the first peace conference was convened at the invitation of Count Mikhail Nikolayevich Muravyov, the minister of foreign affairs of Tsar Nicholas II of Russia. In his circular of January 11, 1899, Count Muravyov proposed specific topics for consideration:

> (1) a limitation on the expansion of armed forces and a reduction in the deployment of new armaments, (2) the application of the principles of the Geneva Convention of 1864 to naval warfare, and (3) a revision of the unratified Brussels Declaration of 1874 regarding the laws and customs of land warfare.

The conference met from May 18 to July 29, 1899; 26 nations were represented. Only two American countries participated, the United States and Mexico. Both conferences failed to deal with disarmament. It was evident that there was no interest in the topic at this time. Basically, the Korean delegates' appeals were not accepted.

Since both of these actions failed, Kim Kojong could not find other mediation alternatives-basically, an impossible situation with the Japanese rule. King Kojong died on January 22, 1919. The Korean government announced funeral services on March 1st, 1919. At this time, the Korean people also planned a huge non-violent demonstration at this funeral service. This demonstration was organized in secret. Japanese colonial rulers thought this was planned by the government and not the people. In response, government leaders were killed.

The Korean independence movement began as nonviolent, nationwide events which developed into violent actions. As a result of the arrest of the first stage leading class, the systematic ideology of nonviolence has been lost to the last leading class. The third state leading class could not reach any agreement with the Japanese government due to Japan's weapons usage to kill participants and enforce other types of violence.

Despite Japan's tyrannical rule and cruelty, the leaders of the third stage continued to protest. Between March and April of 1919, 776 demonstrations for independence took place, of which 486 were nonviolent and 290 were violent. During that time, 7,645 people were killed by Japanese policemen. As a result of the Amritsar Massacre, two large violent demonstrations took place in Mumbai (1921) and Chauri-Chaura (1922). However, due to Gandhi's charismatic nonviolent leadership and nationalistic leaders, Indian participants maintained a nonviolent movement. Gandhi's most influential philosophical principles of nonviolence were sadusatya (truth) and ahimsa (love) as the polar stars of his political zutzisu (nonviolence). Through his fasting, 320-kilometer march, and meditation, he demonstrated these spiritual principles.

The strategies of both nonviolence movements were very similar. They consisted of demonstration marches, prayers, strikes, and boycotts. Between March and May of 1919, 1, 542 demonstrations occurred in 1920, 81 strikes were held. During the 1920s, 199 boycotts were launched with 17,994 workers.[221]

After two nationwide independence movements, both colonial powers temporarily changed their policies as a result of the people's strong protest against the colonial powers' use of violent weapons. This was due to a fear of international massacres. However, Japanese policy was very different from British policy. While Britain's government kept a moderate policy towards India, Japan planned violent policies called culture policies.

<Figure 8>   **Japan 's Violent Actions toward Kore**

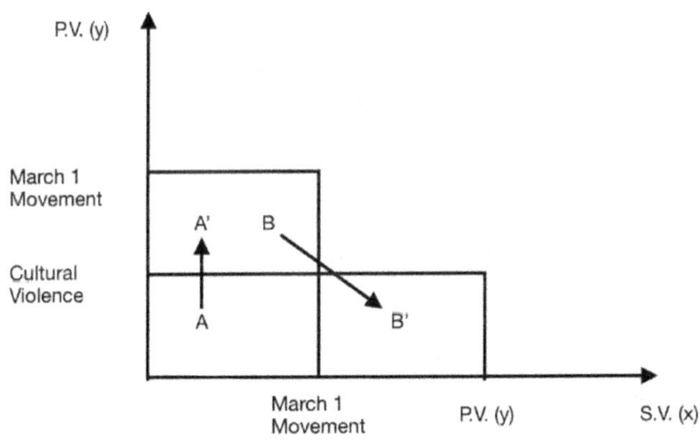

*P.V. = Physical violence line   S.V. = Spiritual violence line

According to <Figure 8>, in the early stage (A, A'), Japan used

---

221 Kang Dong-Jin, "Korean Labors 'Movement under Japanese Colonial Rule," *A Recent Korean History of National Movements,* p.530-531.

a very physical and violent policy to exploit Korea's sovereignty. In the final stage (B, B'), Japan's policy was changed into a spiritual coercion policy to avoid the Korean people's strong protests, and international opinions. The culture policy proved to be more severe than the physical coercion policy. However, in India, the British did not pursue such a spiritual policy.

The most important purpose of Japan's colonial policy was to liquidate Korean nation culture and nation consciousness. In order to avoid national and international criticism, the policy was camouflaged. The Japanese military police system was changed to a general police system. Japan established 751 police stations and increased the number of policemen to 20,750. Japanese policemen arrested many nationalists and demonstrators and killed them through torture. A tentative freedom of speech and education policy has been implemented. Most private schools established by the nationalists were decreased, while technical schools increased to better exploit the material and human resources. Christian schools were temporarily permitted because of international opinion. However, their camouflaged police were immediately uncovered. Japan forced Korean students to learn Japanese language, history, and culture. Through their education policy, they officially prohibited Korean language use in schools and distorted Korean history and culture. The most serious policy was the eradication of Korean thoughts and religions. While Japan encouraged foreign missionaries to evangelize in Korea because of international opinion, Korean Christians were forced to participate in Shinto ceremonies. Many faithful Christians refused to participate in Shinto ceremonies. As a result, 2,000 pastors from all denominations were arrested and approximately 200 churches were closed in 1938 and 1939. The number of Christians decreased from 700,000 in 1938 to 250,000 in 1941.[222] Therefore, according to <Figure 8>, Japan's physical violence policy (A, A') in 1919 was changed into a spiritual coercion policy (B, B') in 1920. This is

---

[222] Andrew C. Nahm, *Korea: Tradition & Transformation*, Seoul, Hollym, 1988 p.289-290.

one of the differences in India's case.

Conclusion:
Results and Significance of the Korean and Indian Independence Movement

Although both countries' people displayed nationwide nonviolent demonstrations, with Korea using some violent demonstrations, the two countries did not achieve their independence until 1945 and 1947 in India's case. As a result of the strong colonial rule in both countries, many people died and their property was lost. However, it is very worthwhile to compare both independence movements 'features that are significant in understanding the formation and transformation of nonviolence movements.

Korean and Indian independence movements share several similarities. Both countries are located in Asia and their movements affected by Asian countries. Korea was affected by the Russian Revolution in 1917 and India by the Korean March First Movement in 1919. Both movements occurred in 1919. Both countries also did not achieve their independence through protests but obtained their liberation through World War II. Both movements were nonviolent movements, even though Korea had some violent protests. In addition, both movements were nationwide movements led by their leading classes.

They also had differences. While both countries were located in Asia, they were suppressed by different colonial powers. Korea was suppressed by Japan, which is located in the same geographic area, and India was suppressed by England, which is located in the western area. Both countries had different social structures. Korea's feudal landowners' class and the lower class were deprived and almost collapsed by Japan. However, India's upper class retained their economic and social positions under

British colonial rule. Nation-structures of the countries differed in their political situations. Under Japanese rule, Korea's national cabinet collapsed, but India's congress existed. The origins of nationwide movements were different from each other. The Satyagraha Campaign in India protested against the Rowlatt Bills, but the March First Movement was not caused by a specific issue. Many nationalistic leaders who stayed in China, America, and Japan with inner nationalists prepared the March First Movement as a huge historical task in 1979. They decided to take solemn action on March 1, two days before Korean ex-emperor Kojong's funeral. This was so as not to excite Japan's suspicions of a nationwide gathering. There was no change in India's leading class during the development of the movement, but Korea's leading class was changed into a grass-roots class which included students. The international opinions of the Korean independence movement were less favorable than those of India's movement. Although Korea had appealed its severe situation to foreign countries secretly including the Paris Peace Conference, held in 1919, Korean people did not get any benefits because Japan forced to boycott it as a member of the peace conference. In addition, Japan did not give any opportunities for negotiations between Korea and Japan's top leaders.

However, both countries' independence movements have historical significance. The Korean March First Movement became an origin of nationwide nonviolence movement in the world. The independence movement of India conveyed an important spirit of national unity to participants. Finally, both movements have greatly affected other countries 'nonviolent and peace movements. The March First Movement spiritually influenced the Chinese May Fourth Movement and the Indian Satyagraha Movement. The spirit and thoughts of the Indian independence movement play a great role in modern nonviolence movements and studies.

<BIBLIOGRAPHY>

Books and articles

Beck, Carl, "Peace Witness Is Mission," *Gospel Herald*, June 1, 1965.

------------, "Students Discuss Peace," *Gospel Herald*, September 7, 1965.

------------, "Korea Workcamp Wins Japanese Friends," *The Mennonite.* September 28, 1965.

------------, "Trek to Korea," *The Mennonite*, November 2, 1965.

------------, "Korean Church Leaders Ponder Peace," *The Canadian Mennonite*, Tuesday, February 22, 1966.

------------, "Korean Talk Reconciliation Hope for Meeting with Japan," The Mennonite, March 15, 1966.

------------, "Japan-Korea Encounter Bring Pleas for Reconciliation," *The Canadian Mennonite, Tuesday,* July 19, 1966.

------------, 'Surprised by Forgiveness Japanese Meet Koreans," *The Mennonite*, October 24, 1967.

Chung-Suk, Chung, "Story of a Korean Boy," *The Mennonite*, September 25, 1962.

Curle, Adam, *Tools for Transformation: A Personal Study*, Hawthorn Press, 1990.

Dyck, Cornelius J., *An Introduction to Mennonite History*, Second Edition, PA, Herald Press, 1981.

Klassen, Jacob M., "Korea's Burden," *The Mennonite*, January 23, 1962.

Kraus, C. Norman, *The Healing Christ: Social Services and The Evangelical Mission*, PA, Herald Press, 1972.

Kyung-Cho, Chung, *Korea Tomorrow: Land of the Morning Calm*, New York: Macmillan Company, 1956.

Leaderarch, John Paul, *Preparing For Peace: Conflict Transformation Across Cultures*, Syrscuse University Press, 1995.

Leatherman, Andrew, "Korean Church Cramps," *The Mennonites*, February 16, 1971.

McGavran, Donald A., *Momentous Decisions in Missions Today*, Grand Rapids:Baker Book House, 1984.

Miller, Robert W., *Diary of Asia Trip*, MCC, Akron, Pennsylvania, March 20-May 1, 1965.

Nahm, Andrew C., *Korea: Tradition and Transformation-A History of the Korean People*, Seoul:Hollym, 1988.

Ro Bong-Rin and Martin L. Nelson. *Korean Church Growth Explosion*, edited Taichung:Asia Theological Association and Seoul:Word of Life Press, 1983.

Shoemaker, J.H., *Notes on Korea's Postwar Economic Position*, New York, I.P.R., 1947.

Sider, Ronald J., *Rich Christians in An Age of Hunger*, Dallas, Word Publishing, 1990.

Spanier, John, *American Foreign Policy Since World War II*, 10th ed., New York, CBS College Publishing, 1985.

Tompkins P., *American-Russian Relations in the Far East*, New York, Macmillan, 1949.

Woo-Keun, Han, *The History of Korea*, Trans. by Lee Kyung-Shik, edited by Grafton K. Mintz, Honolulu, East-West Center Press, 1971.

Yoder, John H., *The Politics of Jesus*, Michigan, William B. Eerdmans, 1972.

Published Reports

The Reports and Statistics for 1964, 1965, presented to the MCC meeting in the annual session of the Hotel Atlantic, Chicago, Illinois, January 15 and 16, 1965.

The Reports and Statistics, MCC, Akron, 1950-1971.

The Annual Report, MCC, Akron, Pennsylvania, 1950-1971.

The Diary of Robert W. Miller's Asia Trip, MCC, Akron, Pennsylvania, March 20- may 1, 1965.

MCC Korea 15th Anniversary Brochure, MCC, Taegu, 1968.

U.S. Department of State Bulletin, Dec. 30, 1945, pp. 1030-1035.

U.S. Department of State, *Korea*, 1945-1948.

The Report of the United Nations Commission on Korea, General Assembly, Official Record, 4th Sess., 1949, Vol.1 (A/936).

Correspondences

Dallas Voran's Letter to J.N. Byler, October 26, 1951.

Dallas Voran's Letter to Glenn Esh, October 26, 1951.

Glenn Hyssong's Letter to the Assistant of Chief of Staff, G-1, October 22, 1951.

Ferd Ediger's Letter to Karl Bartsch, April 16, 1964, found in the file entitled "Japan-Korea Relations," Box 1, File 41, in the "MCC Korean Files, AMC."

Karl Bartsch's Letter to Ferd Ediger, May 1, 1964, found in the file entitled "Japan-Korea Relations," Box 1, File 41, in the "MCC Korean Files, AMC."

Karl Bartsch's Letter to Whom This May Concern, July 6, 1965.

Carl Beck's Letter to Lyle Troyer, July 10, 1965, founded in the file entitled "Japan-Korea Relations," Box 1, File 41, in the "MCC Korean Files, AMC."

Leland Voth's Letter to Carl Beck, August 26, 1965, is found in the file entitled "Japan-Korea Relations," Box 1, File 41, in the "MCC Korean Files, AMC."

Leland Voth's Letter to the Planning Committee, August 26, 1965.

Henry W. Goossen's Letter of Invitation and Guarantee, April 27, 1967, found in the file entitled "Japan-Korea Relations," Box 1, File 41, in the "MCC Korean Files, AMC."

Henry W. Goossen's Letter of Invitation and Guarantee, April 27, 1967.

Henry W. Goossen's Letter of Invitation and Guarantee, May 8, 1967.

Henry W. Goossen's Letter of Invitation and Guarantee, May 10, 1967.

Kim Chun Ihl's Letter to Carl Beck, January 13, 1966, found in the entitled "Japan-Korea Relations," Box 1, File 41, in the "MCC Korean File, AMC."

Lee Dong Keun's Letter to Japan MCC, March 6, 1967, found in the file entitled "Japan-Korea Relations," Box 1, File 41, in the "MCC Korea File, AMC."

Korea Work Camp Conference Director's Letter to Dear Sirs, June 1, 1967, found in the file entitled "Japan-Korea Relations," Box 1, File 41, in the "MCC Korean Files, AMC."

J.R. Dyck's Letter to the Governor of the North Kyung San, May 26, 1969.

Newspapers and Magazine

The Mennonite, 1950-1971.
The Mennonite Weekly Review, 1950-1971.
The Canadian Mennonite, 1950-1971.
"Monthly Aid Helpers 1000 Children," *The Mennonite*, November 9, 1965.
"Couple in Middle Sixties Complete Korea Service Term," in *The Canadian Mennonite*, April 12, 1966.
"Korean Child Care Course 310 Trained in 7 Year," *The Mennonite*, October 13, 1970.
"Korea Child Care Training Program," The Mennonite, May 28, 1963.
"Korea-Japan Reconciliation," *The Canadian Mennonite*, Tuesday, November 1, 1966.

Unpublished reports and brochures
The Report on the Kyung San Vocational School for Orphan Boys Submitted to the United Nations Women's Guild, January, 1955, is found in the "MCC Korean Files, AMC."
The Report on the Kyung San Vocational School for Orphan Boys Submitted to The Asia Foundation, January, 1956, is found in the "MCC Korean Files, AMC."
The Report of MVS Conferences held at MVS, reviewing the present program and suggestions for possible changes on Dec. 1962, is found in the file entitled "MVS Reports 1954-1970," Box 1, File 41, in the "MCC Korean Files, AMC."
MVS Report Operated by MCC Korea, Feb. 27, 1963, found in the title entitled "MVS Reports 1953-1963, Box 1, File 41, in the "MCC Korean Files, AMC."
Japan Mennonite Peace Mission reported by Carl Beck, MCC Japan, Quarterly, July 1 to September 30, 1964, found in the file entitled "Japan-Korea Relations," Box 1, File 41, in the "MCC Korean Files, AMC."
The International Work Camp in Korea, reported by Korea Work Camp Conference, Seoul, 1967, is found in the file entitled "Japan-Korea Relations," Box 1, File 41, in the 'MCC Korean Files, AMC."
Brochure of the Program for Reconciliation Seminar reported by MCC

Korea, October 28-29, 1965, found in the file entitled "Japan-Korea Relations, "Box 1, File 41, in the "MCC Korean Files, AMC."

The 7th Arrangement Committee of Peace Seminar reported by MCC, January 27, 1966, found in the file entitled "Japan-Korea Relations," Box 1, File 41, in the "MCC Korean Files, AMC."

Brief Minutes of the Prayer Meeting (monthly meeting between December 1965 and November 1966), MCC Korea, found in the file entitled "Japan-Korea Relations," Box 1, File 41, in the "MCC Korean Files, AMC."

Brief Minutes of the Report on Seminar: 5th Christian Youth Seminar in Japan, Korea MCC, July 16, 1966, found in the file entitled "Japan-Korea Relations," Box 1, File 41, in the "MCC Korean Files, AMC."

The Recommendation of MVS and Orphans by Kang, Man Choon, found in the file entitled "MVS Reports 1950-1970," Box 1, File 41, in the "MCC Korean Files, AMC."

The MCC Report of Director Foreign Relief and Services on Asia Commissioner Visit, September-November, 1961, p.1, Box 1, File 41, in the "MCC Korean Files, AMC."

The Korea FCA Report, May, 1964, is found in the file entitled "Korea FCA Reports," Box 1, File 41, in the "MCC Korean Files, AMC."

The Paper for Estimating the Future of FCA Community Development Work, found in the file entitled "Korea FCA Reports," Box 1, File 41, in the "MCC Korean Files, AMC."

Korea FCA Budget for 1970 Fiscal Year (1), found in the file entitled "Korea FCA Reports," Box 1, File 41, in the "MCC Korean Files, AMC."

Presented paper at Peace Seminar

Sung-Hyuk Kim, "Re-evaluation of the Korean Family System," presented at the first international peace conference, Taegu, Korea, October 28-29, 1965, found in the file entitled "Japan-Korea Relations," Box 1, File 41, in the "MCC Korean Files, AMC."

Chang-Woo Rhee, "Reconciliation in International Aspect,"

presented at the first international peace conference, Taegu, Korea, October 28-29, 1965, found in the file entitled "Japan-Korea Relations," Box 1, File 41, in the "MCC Korean Files, AMC."

Index

K

R

S

W

X

Y

Z

<APPENDIX>

LIST OF MCC 'S WORKERS (1951-1971)

NO	Name	Activity	Agency	Term
1	Dallas Voran	UNCACK	U/ /	10/27/51- / /52
2	Ernest Raber	MCC Pusan	U/GC/R	07/ /53- / /54
3	Dale Weaver	MCC Taegu	U/OM/R	07/ /53- / /56
4	Robert Lee	MCC Taegu	U/OM/R	/ /53- /27/56
5	Dale Nebel	MCC Taegu	MCC/Japan	/ /53- / /54
6	L. Robert Kohls	MCC Taegu	U/L/R	/ /53- 07/25/54
7	Norma Kohls	MCC Taegu	U/L/R	/ /53- 07/25/54
8	Mrs. Eva Harshbarger	MCC Taegu	U/GC/R	/ / 53- / /54
9	J. Harold Yoder	MCC Taegu	U/OM/R	/ /53- / /55
10	Patrica Yoder*	MCC Taegu	U/OM.R	/ /53- / /55
11	Adam Ewert	MCC Taegu	U/MB/R	10/15/53- / /54
12	Katherine Dyck*	APH Pusan	C/GC/R	10/15/53- 08/ /56
13	Lois Kuhns*	MCC Taegu	U/OM/R	10/15/53-11/ 01/56
14	Howard Burkholder	MCC Taegu	U/OM/P	10/ /53-10/24/56
15	Eldon Warkentin	MCC Taegu	U/EMC/P	10/ /53- / /55
16	Clara Eshleman	MCC Taegu	U/OM/R	/ /54-11/23/57
17	Harry Harms	MCC Taegu	U/OM/P	04/ /54- 02/07/57 / /59- 09/ /62
18	Anna Harms	MCC Taegu	U/OM/R	/ /54- / /62
19	Omar Lants	MCC Taegu	U/OM/R	/ /54- / /55
20	Woodrow Ramseyer	MCC Taegu	C/OM/R	04/ /54-11/ 01/56
21	Merle Springer	MCC Taegu	U/MC/P	/ /54- / /55
22	Valentine Yutzy	MCC Taegu	U/MC/P	02/ /54- 02/07/57
23	Fern Hershberger*	MCC Taejon	U/OM/R	/ /54- 03/27/57
24	Arlene Sitler	Seoul CCF	U/OM/R	/ /54- / /54
25	Donald Klippenstein	MCC Taegu	U/GC/R	/ /55- 07/08/58
26	Betty Klippenstein*	MCC Taegu	U/GC/R	
27	Bertha Kornelson*	PCCH	C/MB/R	/ /55- 08/28/56
28	Margaret Wiens*	PCCH	C/MB/R	/ /55- 09/28/58
29	James Hostetler	Seoul CCF	U/OM/R	/ /54- 12/27/57

30	Helen Tieszen	Seoul CCF MCC Taegu	U/GC/R	/ /54-12/27/57 / /61- / /71 1962-Sabbatical
31	Kenneth Brunk	MCC Taegu	U/MC/R	/ /56- 04/15/59
32	Twila Brunk*	MCC Taegu	U/MC/R	
33	M. Joseph Smucker	MCC Taegu	U/GC/R	/ /56- 07/05/59
34	Katherine Friesen*	SCRH	U/GC/R	/ /56- 09/05/59
35	Robert Gerber	MCC Taegu	U/MC/P	/ /57- 09/12/60
36	Lloyd Miller	MCC Taegu	U/MC/P	/ /57- 03/23/60
37	Leland Voth	MCC Taegu	U/GC/R	/ /57- / /67 1963-Sabbatical
38	Joanne Voth	MCC Taegu	U/GC/R	
39	Arlene Zimmerman*	PCCH	U/MC/R	/ /57- 01/27/60
40	Anna Klassen*	SCRH	C/MB/R	/ /57- 01/27/60
41	Ruth Keim	MCC Taegu	U/OM/R	/ /58- 03/18/61
42	Jacob M. Klassen	MCC Taegu	C/MB/R	/ /58- 09/01/61
43	Katherine Klassen	MCC Taegu	C/MB/R	
44	Daniel Roth	PCCH	U/GC/P	/ /58- 08/29/61
45	Irma Dyck*	PCCH	C/GC/R	/ /59- 03/07/62
46	Tina Letkeman*	PCCH	C/GC/R	/ /59- 03/07/62
47	John Zook	PCCH	U/MC/R	/ /59- 06/30/63
48	Rosemary Zook*	PCCH	U/MC/R	
49	Allen Litwiller	PCCH	U/MC/P	/ /59- 03/07/62
50	Elton Sutter	MCC Taegu	U/MC/P	/ /59- 02/14/62
51	Mabel Brunk*	PCCH	U/OM/R	/03/59- /06/64
52	Esther Thiessen*	SCRH	C/GC/R	/ /59- 07/29/62
53	Roy Bauman	MCC Taegu	C/MC/P	/ /60- 03/29/63
54	Dorothy Hoover*	Pusan CCH	C/BC/R	/ /60- 03/29/63
55	Lydia Schlabach*	Seoul CCF	U/MC/R	/ /60-11/27/63
56	Paul Hochstetler	MCC Taegu	U/MC/P	/ /61-11/30/64
57	Eugene Dick	PCCH	U/GC/P	/ /61-12/02/64
58	Harding Derksen	MCC Taegu	U/GC/P	/ /62- 03/06/65
59	Karl Bartsch	MCC Taegu	C/MB/R	/ /62- 07/30/65
60	Mrs. Evelyn Bartsch	MCC Taegu	C/MB/R	
61	John Slotter	MCC Taegu	U/GC/P	/ /62- 09/29/63
62	Walter Rutt	MCC Taegu	U/MC/R	/ /63- 01/ /65
63	Gladys Rutt	MCC Taegu	U/MC/R	
64	Lyle Troyer	MCC Taegu	U/MC/R	/ /64- 07/ 08/66

65	Leon Sommers	MCC Taegu	U/MC/P	/ /65-11/19/67
66	Mark Miller	MCC Taegu	U/MC/P	/ /65-11/11/68
67	Lloyd Ramseyer	MCC Taegu	U/GC/R	/ /66- / /66
68	Ferne Ramseyer	MCC Taegu	U/GC/R	
69	Henry Goossen	MCC Taegu	U/GC/R	/ /66- / /68
70	Edna Goossen	MCC Taegu	U/GC/R	
71	Gary Marner	MCC Taegu	U/MC/R	/ /67- 04/30/70
72	Sharon Marner	MCC Taegu	U/MC/R	
73	Alfred Geiser	MCC Taegu	U/MC/P	/ /68- 09/ 05/70
74	Andrew Leatherman	MCC Taegu	U/LC/P	/ /68-11/14/70
75	Dorothy Leatherman	MCC Taegu	U/LC/P	
76	John R. Dyck	MCC Taegu	U/GC/R	/ /69-11/24/70
77	Paula Dyck	MCC Taegu	U/GC/R	

SCRH -Seoul Children 's Relief Hospital
Pusan CCH -Pusan Children 's Charity Hospital
APH -Australian Presbyterian Hospital, Pusan
* -Nurse
R -Relief
P -Pax
U -U.S.
C -Canada
MB -Mennonite Brethren,
OM -Old Mennonite
LC -Lutheran Church

Sign-on Letter
March 23, 2001
President George W. Bush
The White House
Washington, DC 20500

Dear President Bush,
As members of the faith community, we are writing to encourage you to take concrete steps toward peace on the Korean peninsula. As your administration reviews its policy toward North Korea, we strongly advocate for continued engagement, as laid out by former Defense Secretary William Perry. Such a process could lead toward normalization of US-DPRK relations and eventual Korean reunification.

Significant advances toward peace have been made in the past several years, most notably last June's historic summit between Chairman Kim Jong-Il and President Kim Dae-Jung. President Kim has made clear his commitment to the "sunshine policy," an approach that you reaffirmed during his visit to Washington earlier this month. North Korea 's response, while still relatively limited in scope, has been nonetheless remarkable after fifty years of enmity. A number of nations, including Canada and some of our European and Asian allies, have already established full diplomatic relations with the DPRK.

We urge you to seize this historic opportunity to end the last remaining conflict of the Cold War era. The military confrontation on the Korean peninsula can best be eased through a negotiated, monitored de-escalation on both sides of the DMZ. North Korea has shown that reductions of tension are also in its interests. Patient, small gestures of goodwill will allow North Korea the political space necessary to respond in kind. These steps could include removal of the DPRK from the State Department's list of terrorist nations, more frequent high-level meetings, changes in the U.S.'s landmine policy, or increased humanitarian assistance, among other possibilities.
By contrast, unilateral moves toward a missile defense system, disregard for the 1994 Agreed Framework or an unwillingness

to negotiate on missile concerns will reverse painstakingly incremental gains, furthering tension and insecurity on all sides. If your administration chooses to pursue the path of diplomacy, you stand an excellent chance of reaching a comprehensive agreement that would render missile defense unnecessary, saving American taxpayers billions and creating an unprecedented degree of security in Northeast Asia.

As citizens and members of faith communities, we believe that we can also play a role in achieving reconciliation and peace. The churches of both North and South Korea have been instrumental in working toward peace and reunification between the two nations. For nearly twenty years, dialogues and consultations have been taking place that have brought Korean Christians from both sides of the border together. U.S. churches, particularly those with significant Korean-American membership, have been active in promoting this dialogue, as well as the critical issue of family reunification. Faith-based groups have also taken the lead in providing humanitarian assistance to victims of famine in North Korea, with demonstrated success in improved nutrition as well as more direct access to all areas of the country.

As the Seoul-based National Council of Churches in Korea has stated, "the way to realize a peaceful order in today's world is to guarantee the security and peace of North Korea, in its relatively difficult position, to cooperate in economic development, and to help North Korea develop amicable relations with other countries without isolating itself from today's changed world order."

We recognize that many problems persist in working with the North Korean government. Yet the consequences for failing to do so are even greater, as North Korea will see little incentive to cease missile production or aggressive military posturing. By contrast, a careful and consistent approach to diplomacy with the DPRK will continue to lead toward long-lasting peace on the peninsula.

Sincerely,

David Radcliff
Director, Brethren Witness
Church of the Brethren General Board

Rev. Michael J. Dodd
Director
Columban Fathers Justice and Peace Office

Martin Garate
Associate General Secretary for International Programs
American Friends Service Committee

Howard W. Hallman
Chair
Methodists United for Peace with Justice

Murray Polner
Chair
Jewish Peace Fellowship

Ken Sehested
Executive Director
Baptist Peace Fellowship of North America

Betsy Headrick McCrae
Program Director for East Asia
Mennonite Central Committee

SangJin Choi
Director
Action for Peace through Prayer & Aid

Rev. Peter Ruggere
Maryknoll Office of Global Concerns

Gary Baldridge

Co-coordinator, Global Missions
Cooperative Baptist Fellowship

Edward W. Stowe
Legislative Secretary
Friends Committee on National Legislation

Asaph Young Chun
President and Founding Chairman
Institute for Strategic Reconciliation, Inc.

Syngman Rhee
President, Presbyterian Churches of USA
Former President, National Council of Churches of Christ in the USA
Chair, International Board of Trustees, Institute for Strategic Reconciliation, Inc.

Inhwa Sohn
President, National Council of Korean Presbyterian Churches of America
Chair, U.S. Board of Trustees, Institute for Strategic Reconciliation, Inc.

Joel J. Heim
Moderator
Disciples Peace Fellowship

Janet Chisholm and Richard Deats
Interim Co-Executive Directors
Fellowship of Reconciliation

Sae Kim
Former President
Korean-American Cultural Center

Sae Park
Treasurer
Korean-American Cultural Center

Bishop C. Dale White
United Methodist Bishop

Juliane Min
Centreville, Virginia

North American MCC/Korea Directors (1951-1971):

Name	Term
Dale Weaver	3/1953-1955
J.N. Byler (interim)	1955
Don Klippenstein	June 1955-June
M. Joseph (Joe) Smucker (interim)	June 1958-July 1959
J.M. Klassen	September 1959-April 1961
John Zook (interim)	1961-1962
Karl Bartsch	1962-1966
Leland Voth (interim)	1965
Lloyd Ramseyer (interim)	1965-1966
Henry W. Goossen	1966-1968
John Dyck	1968-1971

MCC Koreans Employed in Daegu, Pusan and Seoul:

Name	Term
Ahn Bu Young	Interpreter
Chi Dong Yull	Child Care Training
Han You Sook	Child Care Training
Hyon On Gang	Child Care Training
Joo Young Hui	Child Care Training
Kim Un Cho	Assistant to Karl Bartsch
Kwak Shi	Cook for MCC – Taegu
Lee Ae Un (Anna - 1961)	Wife of Harry Harms
Lee Un Shik	Family and Child Assistance
Pak Won Sik	MCC driver
Shim Oo Chun	MCC feeding station supervisor and Interpreter
Suh Il Kyu	Interpreter
Yi In Sul	Child Care Training

MCC/Koreans employed at MVS:

Ahn Doh-Gill – Carpentry teacher, Baek Eel-Jin – Dorm supervisor, Chae Dae-Geun – Printing teacher, Chae Jang-Suk – Hostel manager, interpreter, orphanage director, Chang Yoon-Hee- Assistant to Builder, Mr. Cho – Farm manager, Choi Jung-Shik – Agriculture teacher, Choi Soo-Ryun – Asst. MCSP, Choo Joon-Hoh – Physical education teacher, Chun Gee-Suk – Language teacher, Chung Joo-Kyung – Mennonite Community Service Project, Hyun Soo-Gill – interpreter, orphanage director, Jehshi – Farm laborer (Plowman), Ms. Jung – Choir conductor, Jung Tae-Sun – English teacher, Mr. Kang – Sociology teacher, Kang Im-Won – Metal teacher, Keh Hoon-Chang- History teacher, Kim Byung-Chae(Elder) – Farm manager, Kim Chaang-Soo – Dean, Kim Ee-Bong –Chaplain, Kim Halmony – Cooking and sewing for Kohls, Kim Hun-Gyoo – Carpentry teacher, Kim In-Sup – Agriculture teacher and Dean, Kim Jin-Hong – Chaplain (Retired Pastor, Durae Church in Korea), Kim Kyung-Sun –Kitchen manager, Miss. Kim Mee-Ja, -MVS Accountant, Kim Sang-Bum – Greenhouse manager, Ms. Kim Shill - Music teacher, Kim Sung-Hong – Electronics teacher, Kim Yong-Gill – Language teacher, Kim Yoon-Joo – Mathematics and drafting teacher, Koh Sung-Taek – Mathematics teacher, Kongshi – MVS cook, Mr. Lee – Metal teacher, Lee Dong-Keun – Interpreter, Principal, Lee Hyung-Kon(Elder) – Farm manager 3/1965-10/1970, Lee Jin-Sam – Chaplain, Lee Kyung-Lan- MVS Typist, Lee Shin-Bok-Chaplain, Lee Won-Sang – English teacher (Retired Pastor, Washington Central Korean Presbyterian Church in Fairfax, VA), Lee Young-Doh – MVS Driver, Lee, "Small" – Warehouse keeper, Mr. Lim – MVS driver, Min Byung-Yun – Orphanage director, Moon Hak-Che – Printing teacher, Nam Halmony – Assistant to Cook and sewing, Noh Joong-Goo – Teacher, Oh Young-Suk – Language teacher, Pak(Haraboji) – Dorm supervisor, Pak Boo-Hak – Carpentry teacher, Pak Jae-Bok –

Tailor, Sanjikee Haraboji – Mountain keeper, Shin Yoon-Soo – Interpreter, orphanage director, Mr. Suh – geography teacher, Dorm supervisor, Mr. Whang – Metal teacher, Yoo Kee-Duk (Elder) – Director of grounds and houses, Mr. Yoo – Printing teacher

MVS Graduates Employed by MCC in Korea
-Those graduates who worked for MVS or MCC Office in Taegu (some after military service) are as follows:

 Koh Jung Nam (1st graduate) – MVS Chicken house, Lee Chull-Ong (1st graduate) – MVS Dairy farm, Oh Yong (2nd graduate) – Assistant to Leland Voth, Teacher MVS, 5 years, Cha Chang Eel (2nd graduate) – MVS Chicken house, Lee Sang-Soo (2nd graduate) – MVS Dorm supervisor, Interpreter, Shin Jin Woo (2nd graduate) – MVS Vehicle maintenance, Chung Chung Seok (2nd graduate) – MCC Taegu Office, 6 years, Kim Byung Dong (3rd graduate) – MCC Taegu Office, Yoon Yong-Bong (3rd graduate) – MVS Farm assistant, Kim Jung Soo (3rd graduate) – MVS Dorm supervisor and Hostel Manager in Taegu, Kim Chang-Hoh (Kim Jae-Og) (3rd graduate) – MVS Dairy Farm, Kim Eel-Sahm (3rd graduate) – Translator at MVS, October 1965-January 1969, Chun Dong-Joon (4th graduate) – MVS Vehicle maintenance, Suh Kwang-Eel (5th graduate) – Assistant to MVS purchasing agent and MCC material aid, Lee Jin-Sung (6th graduate) – MVS Dairy Farm, Kim Woo-Shik (7th graduate) – MVS Grounds and houses

ABOUT THE AUTHOR

Sang-Jin (Daniel) Choi

Daniel Choi is a writer, painter, poet, peace activist, and Mennonite pastor who advocates for the homeless and racial harmony. He is the founder of Action for Peace through Prayer Aid (APPA), a member of an NGO that is a special consultative status member of the UN Economic and Social Council (UN ECOSOC) and Dosan Dream International School, Guri City, South Korea.

Daniel Choi opened the House of Peace, a homeless shelter in Washington, D.C. in 1998. One year later, he founded the Fourth Street Community Fellowship, Virginia Mennonite Conference, in the same area in 1999, (which the community called the House of Peace.) A decade later, he started APPA Christian Legal Aid for the poor in 2008.

He served as a member of the advisory council committee for Washington D.C. mayor, 2001-2007. Choi published Peace Times, a newspaper, for fostering ending homelessness and racial harmony, from 1999-2009. In March 2006, he initiated the process of establishing a sister city between Seoul and Washington, D.C.

Daniel Choi has been a representative of GCS international, a member of an NGO that is a consultative status member of UN ECOSOC, created by the International Association of University Presidents. He has been a youth training director for the World Energy Forum, a consultative status member of UN ECOSOC.

In accordance, regarding corporate social responsibility, he has cooperated with the UN Global Compact to develop multitudinous programs and movements such as the UN & NGO leadership training programs, multi-racial harmony, fair-trade movement, ending homelessness, environmental movement, and the UN NGO activities.

In addition to media attention for his ministry efforts, he has received recognition for his unconditional dedication and work to improve international society. Acknowledging his work are numerous individuals and organizations, including a "President Award of South Korea" (Roh, Moo-Hyun Administration) in 2007, former Washington D.C. Mayor Anthony A. Williams, Obama who recognized Daniel Choi's devotion to multi-racial reconciliation with a "Lifetime

Volunteer Service Award" in 2010, and the Russian Government under Boris Yeltsin that granted Daniel Choi a Decoration of International Cooperation in 2011.

He majored in International Public Policy at the Graduate Institute of Peace Studies at Kyung Hee University (Seoul, South Korea). He also studied in the Graduate Program in Conflict Transformation at Eastern Mennonite University (Harrisonburg, VA, USA).

In May 2012, Daniel Choi invited about 30 Mennonite missionaries who served in Korea in the past under the sponsorship of CTS TV, a Korean Christian Television Station. In Gyeongsan, Daegu, the Mennonite missionaries hosted the first reunion in 30–40 years with the disciples they cared for. For elderly missionaries, visiting Korea at that time was the last chance in their lives.

173

A History of Mennonite Workers' Peace Mission   since the Korean War (1951 – 1971)

www.ingramcontent.com/pod-product-compliance
Lightning Source LLC
Chambersburg PA
CBHW070119260726
48658CB00001B/167